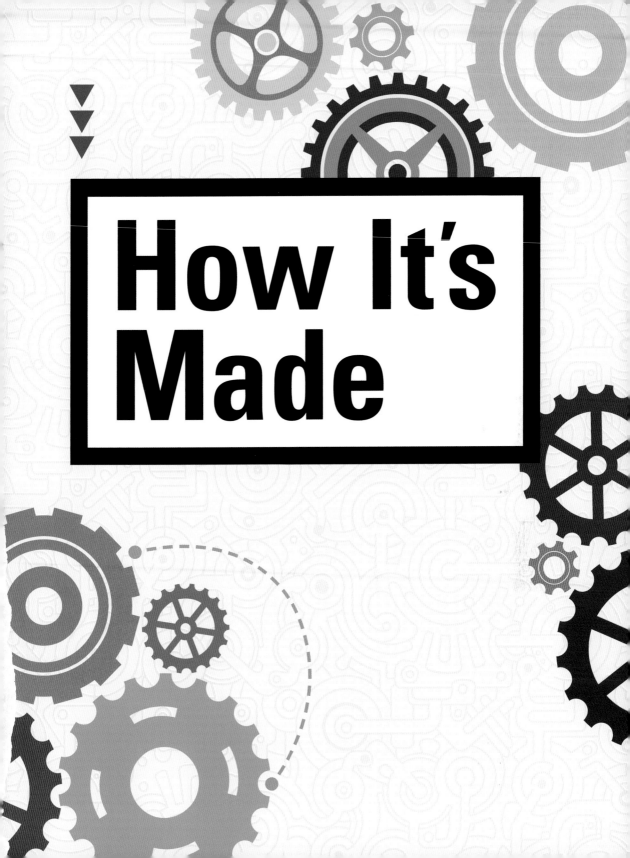

How It's Made

How It's Made

THE CREATION OF EVERYDAY ITEMS

WRITTEN BY THOMAS GERENCER
ILLUSTRATIONS BY MUTI

ABRAMS BOOKS
FOR YOUNG READERS
NEW YORK

Library of Congress Cataloging-in-Publication Data:
Names: Gerencer, Thomas, author.
Title: How it's made / written by Thomas Gerencer.
Other titles: How it is made
Description: New York : Abrams Books for Young Readers, [2022] | Includes
bibliographical references and index. | Audience: Ages 8 to 12 |
Summary: "For 24 seasons and counting, How It's Made has been an
enthralling presence on Science Channel, educating its viewers on the process of making
everything from bread to bifocals and breaking down complex ideas and processes with language
everyone can understand. A "how-it's-made" guide for relentlessly curious kids between the ages of
eight and twelve, this book will teach young readers how the items they love and use every day come
to be, with simple yet captivating descriptions, and full-color illustrations and photographs.
Each chapter will focus on one specific item of particular interest to middle-grade readers,
such as airplanes, candy, or basketballs, and break down exactly what happens at the factory
to make things tick"—Provided by publisher.
Identifiers: LCCN 2021005889 | ISBN 9781419753756 | ISBN 9781647002633 (ebook)
Subjects: LCSH: Manufacturing processes—Juvenile literature.
Classification: LCC TS183 .G46 2021 | DDC 670—dc23

Book design by Celina Carvalho
Illustrations by Muti

p. 4: Plastic beads © Meaw_stocker/Shutterstock.com; p. 5: Injection © Pixel B/Shutterstock.com;
plastic bottle injection machine © Mr.1/Shutterstock.com; plastic bottles © Pixel B/Shutterstock.com;
p. 6: Cutting tool for machining center © Pixel B/Shutterstock.com; p. 7: Spindles © Dmitry Kalinovsky/
Shutterstock.com; Factory © Gorodenkoff/Shutterstock.com; Drill bits © KPixMining/
Shutterstock.com; p. 8: Repair technician soldering © ALPA PROD/Shutterstock.; p. 9: Flux
© ilmarinfoto/Shutterstock.com; An engineer soldering © Serhii Milekhin/Shutterstock.com; Soldering
microcircuit © Niyazz/Shutterstock; p. 10: Engineers © Gorodenkoff/Shutterstock.com;
p. 10: Automotive factory © Evg Zhul/Shutterstock.com; p. 11: Assembling parts © muph/
Shutterstock.com; Welding © Sergey Merzliakov/Shutterstock.com; Car © zentilia/Shutterstock;
p. 12: Welder © Wavebreak Media/Shutterstock.com; Welder with mask © Wavebreak Media/
Shutterstock.com; p. 13: Metal texture © HALCHYNSKA KSENIIA/Shutterstock.com; Tanks with gauge
regulators © Dmitry Kalinovsky/Shutterstock.com; Weld joint © noomcpk/Shutterstock.com;
p. 14: Steel pipe © Vladimir Mulder/Shutterstock.com; p. 15: Tack welding machine © Vladimir Mulder/
Shutterstock.com; Welding machine © Greeneries/Shutterstock.com; Tack welding
© Thor Jorgen Udvang/Shutterstock.com

Printed and bound in China
10 9 8 7 6 5 4 3 2 1

Abrams Books for Young Readers are available at special discounts when purchased
in quantity for premiums and promotions as well as fundraising or educational use.
Special editions can also be created to specification. For details,
contact specialsales@abramsbooks.com or the address below.

ABRAMS The Art of Books
195 Broadway, New York, NY 10007
abramsbooks.com

CONTENTS

INTRODUCTION

How do they make laptops? Gummy vitamins? Screwdrivers? Sometimes we hardly notice all the inventions that surround us, but have you ever wondered where they came from? Vacuum cleaners and frozen pizzas may seem like they were always there, but each one is the answer to a question. How can I clean my floors faster so I can spend more time with family? How can I make a tasty meal in minutes?

So many of the things in your town, your school, your house, and everywhere you go were made to answer similar questions. But every answer had to answer hundreds or even thousands of new questions of its own. How can we make computers small enough to carry? How can we make vitamins chewy? How can we get a plastic handle to stick to a metal screwdriver shaft? For thousands of years, millions of these answers added up to the almost magical world we see around us.

The book you hold in your hands will unlock the secrets of those everyday miracles. It's a VIP pass inside the factories that make sparklers, yogurt, airplanes, and fishing line. You'll see how they manufacture ski boots and basketballs, headphones and clarinets, commercial drones and batteries. You'll find out how they made your mountain bike, the solar panels that light your nights, electric guitars, basketballs, diving masks, crayons, animation, pontoon boats, tap water, and dozens of other bits of ordinary magic. With the answer to the question *How did they make that?* You'll know where the things around you came from. And one day, maybe you'll use that knowledge to answer some new questions of your own.

Ready? Here we go.

COMMON PROCESSES

Every item in this book is made a different way, but most of them didn't completely reinvent the wheel when it comes to how it's made. Here are some common steps that are put together in uncommon ways to make a wide range of stuff.

INJECTION MOLDING

Have you ever wondered how they make the plastic and metal parts in your toys and tools? Many of them are shaped by a process called injection molding. Injection molding is a useful method for shaping different kinds of melted metals and plastics as they cool and harden. Here's how it works:

The factory melts metal or small chips of special plastic called thermoplastic. With thermoplastic molding, the plastic chips start in a hopper.

The chips are pushed down a heated barrel by the threads of a spinning screw. The friction from the threads helps melt the plastic into liquid.

The machine squirts the liquid plastic into a mold. The mold is shaped just like the part the workers want to make. It's made in two parts so it can be opened from the outside.

The plastic cools inside the mold, and then the mold is opened to reveal the newly made part.

MACHINE MILLING

Some parts are made by carving them from solid pieces of metal, wood, or plastic. Many years ago, people had to do this work using hand tools. Today, they use special milling machines. The machines work like this:

The machines have spinning parts called spindles. Workers can attach different tools to the end of the spindle. The tools are something like drill bits.

The spindles spin the tools around, and lower them onto the piece of metal, wood, or plastic that needs to be carved.

The movement of the spindle is most often controlled by a computer. The computer software tells the spindle when to spin, and when and where to lower down to carve the part.

The spindle lowers in different places, using the tool to carve the part into the right shape.

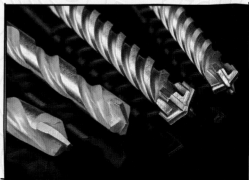

SOLDERING

Soldering is a way to stick together two or more pieces of metal permanently. Here's how it works:

A technician first cleans the two pieces of metal that will be joined together. Any rust, grease, or rough bits must be removed.

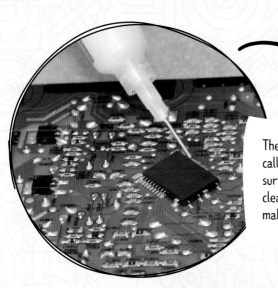

The technician adds something called flux to both metal surfaces. The flux will help to clean the metal. But it also makes the solder stick to it.

Now the tech uses heat to melt a small amount of filler metal—often made of silver, lead, or copper.

The liquid hot solder sticks to the metal surfaces where the flux was applied. The two surfaces now stick together permanently.

FIXTURE ASSEMBLY

When many complicated parts must be connected, workers often use something called a fixture to help them. Here's how fixtures work:

Workers build a frame, called a fixture, out of wood, metal, or other materials.

The fixture's shape fits the shape of the finished part the workers want to make.

The workers assemble the parts of the product they are building on the frame. So far, the parts are not connected. The fixture just provides a sort of skeleton to hang the parts on temporarily.

The parts are all connected, either with glue, rivets, bolts, by welding, or by some other method.

The new part is removed from the fixture. If it can't be removed, the workers take the fixture apart, leaving behind the newly completed part.

WELDING

To join two pieces of metal together in a way that's stronger and longer lasting than soldering, factories often use welding.

They use heat to melt the metal just long enough to fuse the two parts together.

Welders position the metal parts together, often on a fixture.

Sometimes they use a rod of filler metal, melting it to stick together the parts they want to weld. Other times, they only melt a little of the parts they want to weld, and don't use filler.

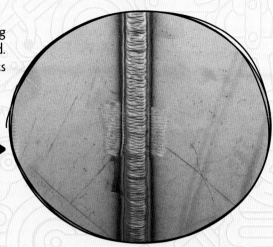

The heat often comes from electricity or from burning gases.

Once the two pieces of metal cool, they're permanently stuck together in a strong, long-lasting bond.

TACK WELDING

Sometimes workers need to hold pieces of metal together just long enough for an automatic welding machine to do its work. They do it with tack welding, like this:

The workers assemble the parts together, often on a fixture.

A welder welds the parts together in a few places—just enough to stick the parts together for a little while. This is kind of like using tacks to hold something in place.

After the tack welding is finished, another welder or more often a welding machine will complete a more thorough welding.

The parts are now permanently stuck together.

FOOD

When you open your refrigerator, you don't just see the food inside. You see the work of thousands of people, and the product of tens of thousands of ideas. Human beings have worked for centuries to make food last longer, taste better, and come in more varieties. Yogurt, sundae cups, and even the simple orange juice on your breakfast table require complex processes to get them into a form we can enjoy. The oldest food we eat? Honey! Let's dig in and find out how factories make some of our favorite foods. Who's hungry?

SUNDAE CUPS

Instant Ice Cream

Who doesn't love an ice cream sundae? You might like yours with nuts or without, with chocolate ice cream or vanilla, with strawberries or chocolate sauce, whipped cream, butterscotch, bananas, strawberries, or all of them at once! But did you know sundaes are actually named after the day that ends the week? The first one popped up in the 1880s, when ice cream sodas were banned on Sundays. Today, you can even get them premade from a store. There's no need to wait.

The sundae factory starts with something called a "white base mix." It's a blend of fresh cream, milk, and sweeteners, mixed up in a shiny steel tank. A worker adds a drizzle of yellow coloring for a richer look. A generous helping of pure vanilla extract boosts the color—and the flavor. Then freezing cold air enters the tank to chill the liquid into soft and tasty ice cream.

A dispenser pumps the right amount of the new ice cream into single-serving sundae cups that move forward on a conveyor belt. Next comes chocolate fudge sauce. Workers mix skim milk and sweeteners, and add large bags of dark, rich cocoa. A paddle blends the mixture, and it's pumped into a plastic **tote** to cool overnight, thickening into rich, velvety chocolate fudge sauce.

When it's ready, the syrup flows from the tote into a big tank, where nozzles squirt it into the cups, on top of the ice cream. Meanwhile, a worker pours another creamy topping blend into a high-speed mixer that beats it to a whipped consistency. Nozzles pump it in on top of the ice cream and syrup.

The chocolate mixture being blended before it is poured into the tote, a container used to transport or store large volumes of liquid.

Now it's time for each cup to get a sprinkling of semi-sweet chocolate chunks. Yum! A conveyor belt sends the cups through an icy blast of air for a quick freeze. Lids slide down a chute and land on top, and automatic rollers press them into place.

A revolving wheel adds plastic collars, and a robot with suction arms grabs six sundaes at a time. It packs them in boxes and seals each with packing tape. Incredibly, this factory makes 1,440 ice cream sundae cups every 15 minutes. We hope you brought a spoon!

Tall tale

The tallest ice cream in history was nine feet tall.

ASIAN NOODLES

Long Food

Noodles were invented in China about four thousand years ago. Since then, cultures around the globe have used them in thousands of unique and tasty dishes. They're fun to eat and packed with energy and protein. They also last a long time, so they're always ready when you want them.

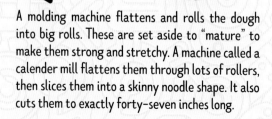

Noodles seem simple. They're just dough that doesn't "puff up"—called **unleavened** dough—squished into different shapes and sizes. But it's not as easy to make them as you'd think.

Noodles always start with flour. In this factory, a technician pours wheat flour and water into a mixer. She adds 80.4 percent flour, 17 percent water, and 2.6 percent salt. Very precise!

A molding machine flattens and rolls the dough into big rolls. These are set aside to "mature" to make them strong and stretchy. A machine called a calender mill flattens them through lots of rollers, then slices them into a skinny noodle shape. It also cuts them to exactly forty-seven inches long.

The noodles are hung to mature again, then steamed to precook them. Then they're cooled and dried, and packaged by hand. The workers in this factory are so good at their jobs that they can bundle the perfect number in a package every time, by eye, without a scale!

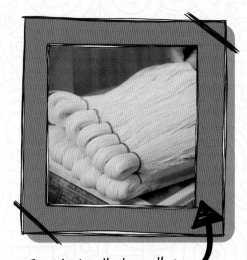

Freshly bundled noodles ready to be packaged!

These noodles will be sold fresh. To make the dry ones you get from a box, the factory dries them in a thermostatic room. Now, where did we put those meatballs?

MAKE YOUR OWN NOODLES

- Combine 1 egg, a pinch of salt, 2 tablespoons milk, 1/2 teaspoon baking soda, and 1 cup flour.
- Knead it into dough and let it rest for 20 mins.
- Cut it into thin strips, dust with flour, and dry for 2 hours
- Cook in hot water for 10 mins.
- Eat with your favorite sauce—yum!

WORDS TO KNOW

Unleavened: Dough made without yeast, baking powder, or any other way to make it "rise."

GUMMY VITAMINS

Chew Your Health

Gummy vitamins were invented by a mom and dad looking for a way to get their daughter to eat healthier. Just like gummy worms, gummy vitamins come in lots of sweet and fruity flavors. They help you fight off colds and flu and build strong teeth and bones, and healthy skin and eyes—not to mention all your other parts.

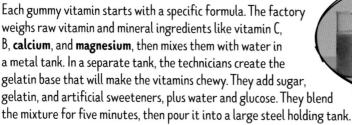

Each gummy vitamin starts with a specific formula. The factory weighs raw vitamin and mineral ingredients like vitamin C, B, **calcium**, and **magnesium**, then mixes them with water in a metal tank. In a separate tank, the technicians create the gelatin base that will make the vitamins chewy. They add sugar, gelatin, and artificial sweeteners, plus water and glucose. They blend the mixture for five minutes, then pour it into a large steel holding tank.

Now the technicians have to test the nutritional mix for contaminants like heavy metals and bacteria. In a laboratory, they squirt samples into a sizzling hot vacuum chamber. A super-hot gas flame called a plasma breaks down metals in the mixture into atoms. A special machine can tell if there are dangerous metals in the mix by looking at the colors of the flame.

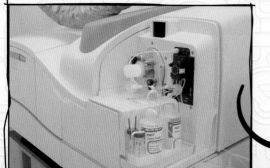

All clear! They add more powdered vitamins to boost the formula's potency. The batter is now ready to be made into thousands of yummy gummy vitamins.

Nozzles squirt the mixture into little vitamin-shaped molds in plastic trays on a conveyor. As the batter hardens, a robotic arm stacks the mold trays in a holding area. Then the arm gently lowers them into place for several hours.

When the vitamins have hardened, they're popped out of the molds and put in a revolving drum. The tumbling action separates each vitamin. They drop onto a conveyor perforated with lots of little holes that let any loose bits fall through. Then the new vitamins cool, harden, and move into a steam chamber. The steam makes them sticky, so another tumbling drum can coat them with tasty, big-grained sugar.

The vitamins funnel into metal chutes where sensors count and sort them into bottles. As the bottles move along conveyors, caps land on them, and spinning rubber mechanisms screw them tightly down. As a last step, the machine sticks labels with product information on each bottle. Depending on the formula, it can take up to three weeks to make a batch of tasty gummy vitamin pills.

Where do vitamins come from?

Some vitamins come from vegetables. Manufacturers get vitamin E from soybeans and vitamin C from rose hip or corn starch. Other vitamins can be made synthetically in laboratories.

WORDS TO KNOW

Calcium: A hard, white mineral that forms the building blocks of bones and teeth.

Magnesium: An essential mineral that plays a vital role in nerve and muscle function.

TAP WATER

Modern Miracle

Have you ever stopped to think how magical tap water is? You turn a handle, and out pours clean, clear water for bathing, brushing your teeth, or grabbing a cool drink on a hot day. But it wasn't always like that. In the days before tap water, people had to live near water sources or have it brought to them through backbreaking labor. Let's take a look at where your water comes from and what happens to it before it gets to your faucet.

This water starts its journey to the treatment plant by flowing from a river through a metal grille that keeps out large debris, like tree branches. From there, it flows to a pumping station, where a giant revolving screen removes fish, garbage, and grass. A pump moves this dirty, smelly **raw water** to the treatment plant.

The first tank holds a chemical called **aluminum sulfate**. It acts as a **coagulant**—a substance that thickens liquid into globs. In the raw water, the globs are sticky and called **flocs**. Bacteria, mud, and other impurities stick to those flocs.

There, technicians add a powerful form of the chemical element carbon, called **activated carbon**. It absorbs contaminants like solvents and pesticides. Then the water flows through a series of mixing tanks.

The second tank holds a chemical polymer and super-fine particles of sand, called micro-sand. The polymer coats the sand, making it stick to the flocs. In the next tank, the heavy flocs settle to the bottom. Now the water is clear, but far from drinkable because it's full of bacteria, viruses, and other organic matter.

The water trickles into a filter, passing through a layer of anthracite—a type of coal—and a layer of sand. This filters out remaining particles. The workers then add a small amount of chlorine to kill bacteria and other nasties, and **silicon** to prevent calcium buildup from blocking our water pipes.

A government inspector checks the water to make sure the chlorine level doesn't pass twenty-millionths of an ounce per liter.

It takes about forty-five minutes to turn raw water into treated water. Then electric motors pump it through underground pipes right to your faucet.

DID YOU KNOW?

The first water pipes were constructed in India, almost six thousand years ago.

WORDS TO KNOW

Activated carbon: Charcoal processed to create small pores that let it absorb chemicals and other contaminants.

Aluminum sulfate: A chemical compound made of aluminum, sulfur, and oxygen, with the chemical formula $Al_2(SO_4)_3$. It dissolves in water and is used as a coagulant in drinking-water treatment.

Coagulant: A chemical compound that makes invisible particles in water cling together to form more manageable clumps.

Floc: A clump of contaminants made by adding a coagulant to water.

Raw water: Water before it's treated and processed for drinking. It may be full of living organisms and debris.

Silicon: An inert mineral found in quartz and beach sand.

ORANGE JUICE

Drinkable Fruit

No one knows who came up with the idea of squeezing oranges to make juice. It's yummy, sweet, easy to pour, and makes a great sidekick for your cereal or bacon and eggs. Today, millions of people start their day with a tall glass of OJ.

Orange juice starts in farms of planted fruit trees called groves. The fruit takes several months to grow, then gets picked by hand in early November. An automated picking system could damage the trees and fruit. This farm grows a small, juicy type of orange called a Hamlin orange. Hamlin trees grow lots of fruit and stand up well to the cold.

Pickers pluck the juice-packed fruit when it's green on the outside, but sweet on the inside. They put it in a big, soft bag and take it to a processing facility. A chute rolls the oranges downhill to a washing station, where sprayers and spinning brushes scrub them clean. A conveyor takes them up under some big fans to dry them. The oranges are checked for damage several times during this process.

Juicing machine teeth about to squeeze the juice of an orange!

Gentler brushes scrub off the remaining dirt, and the oranges fall off the conveyor and into a bin. A worker feeds them into a juicing machine that uses metal teeth to peel the skin. The machine squeezes the juice out, screening out seeds and thicker pieces of pulp. Then the juice flows into a vat, where another screen lets in just the right amount of pulp. Some pulp? More pulp? Most pulp? No pulp? Whatever one you like best, there are different filters to make it perfect.

The juice gets bottled in plastic jugs, then immediately chilled. Since the company doesn't heat the juice, it won't last long, but it makes up for a short shelf life with bursting flavor and a deep orange color. Now if we can just find those pancakes . . .

DID YOU KNOW?

One glass of orange juice has 67 percent of the recommended daily intake of vitamin C, plus other vitamins and minerals like folate, potassium, and magnesium.

HONEY

Bee Sweet

What's all the buzz about honey? This fascinating food has been around for millions of years—long before Pop-Tarts, breakfast cereal, or the human race. As long as it's kept in airtight containers, honey never spoils. In fact, scientists have found three-thousand-year-old honey in Egyptian pyramids—and it was perfectly edible! The average beehive can make up to one hundred pounds of honey every year. But what's the secret behind this awe-inspiring apiarian treat?

Honey starts in a field, of course, where special forager bees sip nectar from flower blossoms. They store it in nectar sacs inside their bodies and fly back to the hive, where honey-maker bees suck it out and chew it. The chewing breaks down the nectar's complex sugars into simple sugars called **glucose** and **fructose**.

The worker bees squirt the chomped-up nectar into honeycombs made of six-sided—or hexagonal—cells made out of wax. They fan it with their wings, evaporating its water in the warm air of the beehive. That shrinks it down, making it into thick and gooey honey. The bees cap each honey-filled cell with wax. That's when the beekeeper steps in.

A honeycomb full of bees, including the queen!

To keep the bees from stinging, the beekeeper sprays the hive with smoke from burning pine needles. Why does that work? Because when a beehive is attacked, bees give off a special smell called an alarm **pheromone**. That tells all the other bees it's time to sting. The smoke blocks the bees' sense of smell. It also mimics a forest fire, so they suck up honey to get ready for a flight to safety. The extra honey weight makes them sluggish, so they don't attack.

The beekeeper also puts a smelly new cover on the hive called a bee escape. It smells like cherries. You might like that smell, but bees think it stinks, so they fly to the bottom of the hive to get away. Another spray of smoke, and the beekeeper removes the bee escape. Now *he* can escape with the honeycombs. The bees make these in easy-to-carry frames the beekeeper put in the hive earlier.

Inside the honey-processing facility, he puts the honeycomb frames on an uncapping machine. Like a razor, it shaves the wax caps off the honey-filled cells. Workers scrape off extra wax, then set the frames on a machine called a honey extractor. It spins the honeycombs, forcing honey from the cells. Then they filter the honey and bottle it for selling.

Honeycombs about to go for a spin on the honey extractor!

When the factory has more honey than they can sell, they let it **crystallize**. That turns it white and hard so they can store it for a long time without worrying that it will spoil. When they get more orders, they heat it up to turn it back to sweet, gold, liquid honey.

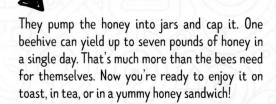

They pump the honey into jars and cap it. One beehive can yield up to seven pounds of honey in a single day. That's much more than the bees need for themselves. Now you're ready to enjoy it on toast, in tea, or in a yummy honey sandwich!

Busiest Bee

A hive can house hundreds of thousands of bees, all the children of a single queen bee. The queen lays up to two thousand eggs a day, creating the workforce needed to feed and protect the colony.

Beeswax treat

Sometimes, the factory slices the wax honeycomb into pieces with a heated knife. They bottle it as is and sell it, and you eat it, wax and all. Yum!

Waste not

The beeswax lining of the honeycomb goes to other factories that use it to make candles, furniture polish, lipstick, and other products.

WORDS TO KNOW

Apiarian: Having to do with beekeeping.

Crystallize: To turn into durable crystals.

Fructose and **glucose:** Simple sugars that are easily processed into energy in the bloodstream.

Pheromones: Special chemicals that create a unique odor, sending messages to other animals of the same species. Some pheromones can tell bees to attack.

FISH FARMING

Underwater Livestock

If you love eating fish like grilled or broiled salmon, you might be surprised to know a lot of it comes from farms. Fish farms handle about 20 percent of the world's fish production. Some fish farms are high-tech, while others use old-fashioned methods. Get along, little doggie!

To get two fish to mate, a fish farmer presses on the belly of a female fish and squeezes out her eggs. A one-pound fish has about one thousand eggs. Whew! But it only takes about a minute to get them out.

Next, he squeezes sperm out of a male fish—no microscopes or test tubes. The farmer mixes the eggs and sperm by hand, then rinses them with water. He repeats this step seven or eight times until the water runs clear.

He tosses out the eggs that float, because if they float, that means they're duds. He puts the good eggs in bottles, filling them with water. They'll **incubate** for about a month. When they've finished incubating, the farmer empties the bottles and spreads the eggs on a slatted surface. They lie there underwater for ten to fifteen days. When they hatch, the baby trout swim down through the slats into a basin.

The baby trout feed off their **yolk sacs** for the first eighteen days. After that, they eat special trout food made from fishmeal.

They grow about eight inches long during the next eight months. At that size, the smaller trout around them start looking pretty tasty. So the farmer has to move them to separate basins so they don't become a snack.

It takes about 1.5 years until these fish are fully grown. Then the farmer moves them to a human-made lake. From here, the fish will go to market. But before they leave, there's one last step—the farmer mates them, continuing the circle of life.

Fish farm facts

- The adult fish in this farm eat brown shrimp.
- Fish farming began in 2000 BCE.
- By day twenty-five, if an egg is alive, two little black dots appear. Those are the fish's eyes.

WORDS TO KNOW

Yolk sac: A temporary organ that delivers nutrients to an embryo.

Incubate: To keep an egg at a warm, stable temperature so the animal inside can develop and hatch.

YOGURT

Symbiotic Snack

Did you know your yogurt is alive? Well, part of it is, anyway. Yogurt is one of the healthiest foods you can eat, yet it's chock-full of bacteria. But these bacteria are good for your tummy. They help you turn food into energy, and get all the vitamins in your breakfast to your bloodstream.

The first step in making fruit-flavored yogurt is to check the fruit. Workers toss out pits and cut off bruised parts. Then they chop the fruit and mix in water, flavors, colors, and ingredients called stabilizers that make it smooth. Next comes sugar in a heated mixer.

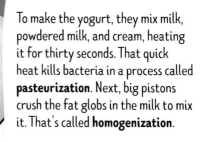

To make the yogurt, they mix milk, powdered milk, and cream, heating it for thirty seconds. That quick heat kills bacteria in a process called **pasteurization**. Next, big pistons crush the fat globs in the milk to mix it. That's called **homogenization**.

The real magic comes next. The mix enters gently heated **fermentation** tanks, and workers pour in packets of live bacteria! This special bacteria, called *Lactobacillus acidophilus*, grows naturally in your tummy. It also grows in the yogurt—for six to twenty hours depending on the type.

The yogurt being filtered into its container. This machine has only filtered air to prevent contamination.

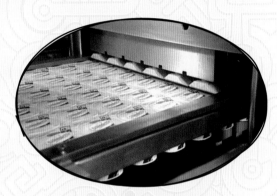

Now a machine heats sheets of plastic, molding them into containers for the finished yogurt. It quickly labels them, and another machine fills them with yogurt and fruit. To protect the yogurt from contamination, the air in the machine is temperature-controlled and filtered. Last, the machine heat-seals the containers with foil covers. Now they're ready for your breakfast. Time to grab a spoon!

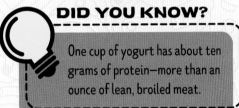

DID YOU KNOW?

One cup of yogurt has about ten grams of protein—more than an ounce of lean, broiled meat.

WORDS TO KNOW

Fermentation: Growing healthy bacteria in food to improve its taste, shelf life, and nutrition benefits.

Homogenization: Crushing fat droplets in milk so they don't later separate and float to the top.

***Lactobacillus acidophilus*:** A bacteria found in human intestines that plays a vital role in human health, including balancing potentially harmful bacteria.

Pasteurization: Heating milk or other foods briefly to kill bacteria.

FROZEN PIZZAS

Party Time All the Time

Crunchy, chewy, hot, and bursting with zesty flavor, pizza is a crowd pleaser for hungry people of all shapes and sizes. Millions of pizzas travel daily from the frozen foods aisle in the supermarket to the dinner table. They're ready in minutes, but how do they taste so fresh when they start out so frozen?

Frozen pizzas start with a maze of machines that make the dough. Workers blend flour, salt, sugar, water, yeast, and oil into a large mixer, tossing in a bit of cornmeal. The mixer is powerful—driven by a truck transmission! The dough gets set aside to rise, then a "chunking machine" divides the big blob into smaller chunks.

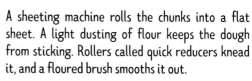

A sheeting machine rolls the chunks into a flat sheet. A light dusting of flour keeps the dough from sticking. Rollers called quick reducers knead it, and a floured brush smooths it out.

FOOD FOOD FOOD FOOD FOOD

Next, stainless steel spikes prick the dough with little holes, to keep it from making big bubbles in your oven. A plastic roller with round ridges cuts out hundreds of round pizza shapes. A conveyor takes these new crusts to an oven, where they bake for two minutes at high heat.

DID YOU KNOW?

Americans eat about one hundred acres of pizza every day.

Next stop—tomato sauce. While the crusts move down a conveyor belt, a curtain of rich, red sauce falls on the crusts from a tank above. A cheese machine adds shredded mozzarella, and another machine sends down a waterfall of pepperoni, sausage, and other toppings. Then a freezer called a blast cell freezes them rock-hard.

Another machine wraps the newly frozen pizzas in clear plastic, and a vision control system takes a picture of each one to look for problems. If it spots an imperfection, it blasts the less-than-perfect pizza into a rejects tub with a jet of air. Meanwhile, a mechanical arm pushes each finished pizza into a waiting box. Dig in!

GUMBALL MACHINES

Gum on the Go

The first gumball machine showed up in 1907 on a New York City subway platform. Today, gumball machines are everywhere. Pop in a coin, turn a knob, and out comes a brightly colored, chewy treat.

To make a gumball machine, a worker ladles molten **zinc** into a holding furnace. A steel plunger pushes the free-flowing metal through a shape called a **die** to create the machine's heavy, metal base. A mechanical claw puts the part on a conveyor belt to cool. Other dies shape the coin mechanism, handle, and drive gears.

To make the gumball chute, a worker pours piping hot liquid aluminum into a mold. He heats the mold with a gas flame to stop water droplets from condensing, which would wreck the metal's shape. Even though he's heating it, the mold is still cool enough to harden the aluminum in seconds.

Next, workers use a machine called a punch press to trim waste from the parts. A computerized tool cuts a hole in the top of the shatterproof plastic globe that will eventually hold the gumballs.

Another worker assembles the coin mechanism. She screws together the front plate, coin carrier, back plate, and a turning part called a **cam**. She adds the knob that turns the coins, and gives it a quick test by popping in a coin and turning it. People all over the world like gumballs, so the coin mechanism can be adjusted to accept lots of different sizes.

Now they spray powder paint on the machine's lid and bake it. Baked powder paint is chip-resistant and can stand up to a beating in a busy store.

Then it's time to put it all together. They cover the dispensing wheel with a part that keeps free gumballs from spilling out. Rats! Next comes an adapter ring, the plastic gumball globe, and an aluminum top ring. They slide rods through to hold everything in place. Then they add a plastic body to the base, and the chute door and cover. They mount the coin mechanism, lock the lid on, and they're done. I hope I get a blue one. You?

Pop your ears

Have you ever been on a plane and chewed gum to get your ears to pop? Chewing gum makes you swallow more, because it makes your salivary glands squirt out 250 percent more saliva. The extra swallowing helps release the pressure in your ears.

Gumballs ready to be dispensed!

WORDS TO KNOW

Cam: A rotating part often used to change rotary motion, where an object rotates around a fixed point, into linear motion, where an object follows a straight line.

Die: A special tool used to shape materials like metals in a manufacturing process. Toy metal cars are made from dies, or "die-cast."

Zinc: A metal used widely in manufacturing because of its excellent castability, durability, and corrosion resistance.

3

SPORTS

Take me out to the ball game—or the court, lake, ocean, or ski mountain! *Billions* of people watch, play, and obsess about their favorite sports every day. But whether baseball, basketball, or some other go-getting activity is your thing, you'll need gear to make it happen. From baseballs to wet suits to Foosball tables, let's peek at how some of our favorite sporting gear is made.

FOOSBALL TABLES

Portable Soccer

Gooooaaal!!! Table soccer was first patented by a British inventor in 1923. It caught on like wildfire across Europe, with leagues forming by the 1950s. A decade later, an American working in West Germany fell in love with the game. He brought it to the United States, using the German word for it: "Foosball."

Foosball tables like the one you see here start at a **foundry**, where workers melt down bars of aluminum. An **injection molder** shoots the molten metal into player-shaped molds. Each mold makes four sizzling-hot players.

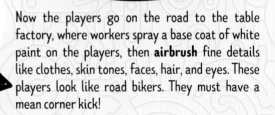

A worker puts each **casting** on a press and separates the players from one another with a single strike. Then a computer-guided tool drills a hole for the rod that will hold the players up.

Now the players go on the road to the table factory, where workers spray a base coat of white paint on the players, then **airbrush** fine details like clothes, skin tones, faces, hair, and eyes. These players look like road bikers. They must have a mean corner kick!

The workers build the table from solid beech wood. They use a computer-guided **milling machine** to shape the parts, drill holes, and engrave the company name. They put the table's sides together with bolted steel rods and glue, then add wood panels and support bars. They either stain the wood or leave it natural, depending on what kind of table they decide to make. Then they add a finish coat of clear varnish.

We're almost FIFA-ready, but we need a ball-return panel to roll the ball down to an aluminum tray after each score. The workers add that, then add a plywood table bottom, aluminum goal nets, and scoring markers to keep you and your friends honest while you play. Next they add the wood-and-vinyl playing field, because AstroTurf would be too grippy.

The workers put on wooden trim and bolt the players to the holding bar. A rubber bumper at each end of the bar protects the side walls from adrenaline-packed play. Workers then feed a thinner steel rod into the bar to make it **telescopic**. Last, they protect the table's top edge with plastic trim and add four sturdy wooden legs. Anyone for league play?

WORDS TO KNOW

Airbrush: An air-operated brush that sprays paint for precision work.

Casting: An item made from metal by melting it, pouring it into a mold, and cooling it.

Foundry: A special type of factory where workers melt metal and pour it into shaped containers called dies.

Injection molding: The process of injecting metal or liquid thermoplastic into a mold to shape it.

Milling machine: A device that rotates a tool to cut and shape a piece of wood or metal.

Telescopic: Having multiple parts, one inside the other, to allow an object to get longer or shorter by pulling or pushing it.

DIVING MASKS & FINS

Mermaid Mods

To see underwater, you need a layer of air between your eyes and the lake or ocean that you're swimming in. Without the air inside a mask, your eyes can't focus, and fish or sunken pirate treasure will look blurry. Fins help your underwater adventures too, by pushing extra water when you kick. Between the two, you're a little like a human dolphin—or a mermaid.

Fins have two parts—a foot pocket and a water-pushing blade. Both are made of heat-shaped plastic called **thermoplastic**. To melt the plastic into liquid, workers mix tiny clear bits of it together with colored-dye bits and drop them in the feed tank of an injection molder.

The molder melts the granules, then injects the hot, liquid plastic into a hole shaped like the part the workers want to make. When the mold opens, a robot grabs the fin blade using suction. It puts the blade on a conveyor, where it rides through a chilly tunnel, hardening as it cools. Another injection molding machine adds more details like side walls and a foot pocket in a process called **overprinting**.

The deepest human dive is 1,082 feet, accomplished by diver Ahmed Gabr. At that depth, Gabr's mask had to withstand the pressure of a full-grown tiger on every inch!

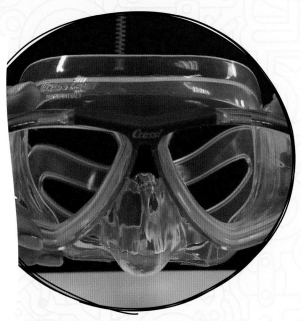

We're not ready for the Mariana Trench yet, because we need a mask. It's made from a flexible **silicone** skirt attached to a stiff plastic frame that holds glass lenses in place. The mask's skirt gets molded out of silicone. Unlike thermoplastic, which turns liquid as it cools, silicone starts out as liquid and is then heated to harden it. A worker assembles the mask by feeding a silicone head strap through the frame's buckles, then attaching the skirt and lenses to the frame. Finally, she clips in rigid parts to hold the lens in place. Now we're ready for the deeps.

WORDS TO KNOW

Overprinting: Adding more plastic parts to an injection-molded product.

Silicone: A rubber-like type of plastic used in lubricants and soft products like cooking utensils or diving masks.

Thermoplastic: A kind of plastic that can be melted and cooled to form multiple shapes. Used in injection-molding machines during the manufacturing process.

WET SUITS

Underwater Warmth

The first wet suits weren't a hit with divers, swimmers, and surfers. They were hard to put on and rubbed the skin raw. But when the surf's up and the temperature is down, today's comfy neoprene wet suits can keep you toasty and happy while you're swapping flips with the sea life.

Wet suits fit like a second skin, so many wearers have theirs custom made. To make a custom-fitted wet suit, a tailor measures the person who will wear it from neck to ankles. A worker cuts out cardboard patterns, using them to snip out the shapes that will become sleeves, legs, and the wet suit's body from a sheet of **neoprene**. More than fifteen pieces fit together like a scuba-diver-shaped jigsaw puzzle.

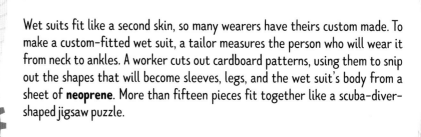

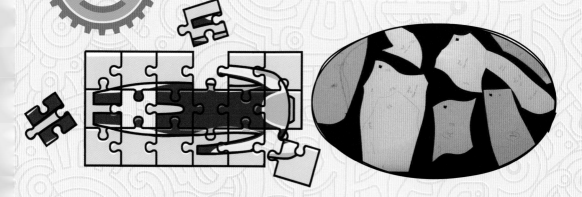

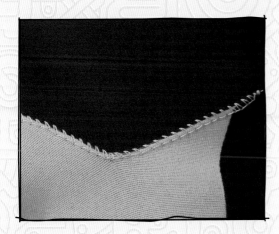

Using a hot press, the workers heat the pieces to expand them. They press a decal of the manufacturer's logo on one piece, then spread waterproof glue along the edges. They press the glued edges of the parts together, using paper to protect the places they don't want to stick. When it's dry, a seamstress stitches everything together with a curved needle that goes in only partway, then comes back out on the same side. This halfway-through stitching is called blind stitching, and it ensures a more watertight seal.

It's almost Neptune time. The workers seal the seams with a hot roller and some **nylon** tape. A nozzle blows hot air to activate the tape's sticky adhesive. They sew a plastic zipper to the back and add a Velcro stopper to prevent unzipping. Then they glue a waterproofing panel near the zipper and the wet suit is ready to take you to the bottom of the sea.

How do wet suits work?

A wet suit lets a small amount of water seep between it and your skin. Your body warms this watery layer to trap heat inside.

Making neoprene

Making neoprene is a bit like baking a cake. Different chemicals are mixed in a reaction that makes small synthetic chips. Workers melt the chips like chocolate, mixing in colors and foaming agents. Then they bake it in a special oven. Mmm, rubbery!

WORDS TO KNOW

Neoprene: A stretchy, insulating fabric used to make wet suits and other soft, water-resistant items.

Nylon: A soft material that can be melted and worked into fibers, shapes, and wraps.

BASKETBALLS

Slam Dunk

A lot happens when you slam a basketball into the ground. The rubber stretches, flattening a little. The air inside compresses too. Then the squished-down air and rubber suddenly snap back, making the ball bounce up into the air.

At the ball's core is an inflated rubber **bladder**. To make it, a factory worker folds a sheet of natural rubber—made from the gooey sap of rubber trees—into a special shape. He cuts and seals the ball with a press, then glues a plug in its hole. Like magic, the ball will now hold air.

Another worker pumps up the bladder in a heated chamber, **curing** it. Then the ball spins on a revolving bar, wrapping up in nylon threads that strengthen it and keep it round.

Just a few more steps until we're ready for the court. Workers make the ball's outside by mixing rubber, synthetic rubber, a kind of salt called **magnesium carbonate**, and oil. They roll the freshly made rubber into sheets, cure it, and fold it. A machine rolls and flattens out the folded rubber, and then a cookie-cutter-like tool punches out a lot of fish-shaped strips.

A worker puts some of these strips into a bonding chamber shaped like the outside of a basketball. She puts the bladder in and pumps it up. Airball! Inside, heat and pressure mash the bladder and the strips together. Instant basketball.

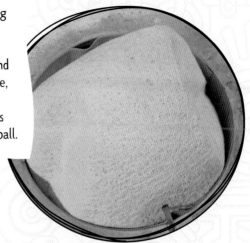

Another hot mold stamps a pattern and a logo on the ball, and a worker paints black rubber stripes and adds a fill-valve to control the air flow when you pump it up. For now, mechanical fists squeeze the air out for packaging, and a worker wraps the ball in plastic and ships it to the store. It only took a couple hours to make this basketball, but it's ready to bounce back for years to come.

It takes all kinds

This factory also makes other balls, like volleyballs and medicine balls. Each type of ball gets its own pattern and colors of rubber.

WORDS TO KNOW

Bladder: A sack or bag made from stretchy manufactured material that can grow larger as it's filled with air or liquid.

To cure: To preserve or harden meat or material by various methods, including heating, salting, or drying.

Magnesium carbonate: A white, solid, inorganic salt with the molecular formula $MgCO_3$.

BASEBALLS

Out of the Park

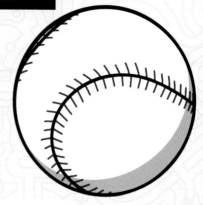

A total of 300,000 home runs have been hit in Major League Baseball since 1901. Not one of those could have happened without the mighty baseball. Each ball is built precisely to league standards that date back to 1872—just seven years after the end of the Civil War! When you hold a baseball, you're literally holding a piece of history in your hand. The balls are all the same weight and size—five ounces and nine inches around. Without these exacting standards, we couldn't compare one home run to another.

In the ball's heart is something called the pill—a round cork sphere with a red rubber casing, smaller than a golf ball. Workers pour **latex** glue over hundreds of these pills inside a metal drum. Rollers spin the drum so each one gets an even coat. The glue won't dry completely, so the pills stay sticky to the touch.

A machine spins each pill to wrap it in a layer of four-ply wool. By the way, you're getting a rare glimpse inside this top secret factory. This is the first time a camera has ever taken pictures of this classified machine.

The workers wind more wool around the pills—three-ply this time—and then still more, with lighter yarn. The layers give the ball its elasticity, so it springs back after you nail it with a bat. One last layer, this time of poly-wool blend, gives it a smooth surface.

The fully wound pill is called the center. The workers weigh and measure it, then coat it with more glue in another spinning drum. This time, the wool absorbs the glue, sticking the many strands together.

Before you can blow the cover off *this* ball, workers have to put it on. A press punches figure eights from a leather sheet, complete with holes around the edge. Workers stamp each with a date and **lot number**, then wrap them with wet towels to make them soft enough to sew.

The center ready to be glued and covered!

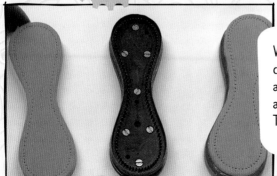

Workers roll glue on the insides of the leather covers, then press two around a sticky center. It's a perfect fit. They clamp the two pieces in a vise and **cross-stitch** them together with two needles. Then they rub the thread with wax to stiffen it.

When it comes to cross-stitching, these workers are in a league of their own. They make quick work of the 108 stitches in each ball. There are 350 sewing workers in this factory, making eight to ten *thousand* balls per day. That's quite the batting average!

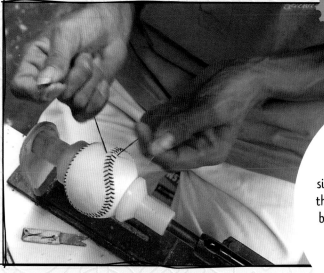

The final stitch goes through the middle of the ball and out the other side. Then the sewing worker pulls the stitches into a familiar V shape before a press smooths them out. Smoother balls are harder to grip and make pitching more challenging for the pros.

Last, a three-headed stamper gives each ball a trademark, league logo, and commissioner's signature. It takes a full week to make one, but every one is a grand slam.

Where does cork come from?

Cork is a waterproof, floating material that grows in the bark of special trees called cork oaks. The trees are found mostly in Europe and Africa and take twenty-five years to grow. That's a long inning, but thankfully we don't have to kill the trees to strip their cork.

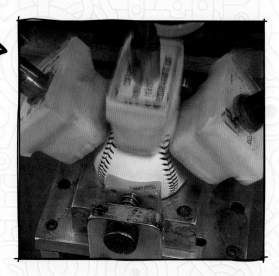

How hard does a bat hit?

In the MLB, a fastball traveling 90 mph can fly from the bat at 110 mph. The collision between bat and ball lasts only a thousandth of a second. The bat hits the ball with about 4,145 pounds of force.

WORDS TO KNOW

Cross-stitch: An X-shaped stitch that makes a stronger bond than a single, one-way stitch.

Latex: A white, milky fluid made from the seeds of plants like milkweed, then processed into a stretchy, rubber-like material.

Lot number: A number given to each batch, or lot, of a product in a factory. Lot numbers help manufacturers trace defects.

SKATEBOARD WHEELS

Rad and Round

If you've ever carved a fakie or worked a 5-0 grind, you owe a lot to skateboard wheels. Without their smooth and grippy glide, a kickflip or an ollie would slam your knees and be almost impossible to land.

These colorful skateboard wheels start with a design on a computer. Then, software-guided tools use that design to carve two halves of wheel molds from aluminum pucks. Workers put the metal halves together, and a nozzle squirts synthetic rubber called **polyurethane** into the space between them. The rubber hardens fast and then workers bake the mold to zap any bubbles, leaving a solid piece of rubber inside.

The workers blast air through the mold and around the wheels to pop them out. Then an automatic cutter spins the wheels on a lathe to give the edges a nice, smooth, rounded shape.

To make these wheels a little gnarlier, an artist prints a **film negative** of a design and puts it on a printing plate. It's coated with a special photographic chemical known as an **emulsion**. He flips on an ultraviolet light, and the image burns onto the plate. Another chemical etches the image deeper in the metal. Then a printing machine spreads ink on the metal and uses it to stamp the picture on the wheel with a big stamp. Elapsed time? About three days. Ready for a ton of grinds, grabs, and kickflips.

DID YOU KNOW?

Skateboarding was first called sidewalk surfing. Early boards were rectangular with steel or ceramic wheels that were a lot harder to control.

WORDS TO KNOW

Film negative: An image on a sheet of transparent plastic, used to create a photograph when light shines through it.

Photographic emulsion: A light-sensitive substance that reacts with other chemicals to transfer an image from a film negative to another object.

Polyurethane: An organic polymer used in paint and flexible plastic products.

SKI BOOTS

Downhill Kicks

A hundred years ago, skiers wore regular hiking boots and held them on their skis with leather straps. Look out below! But modern ski boots clamp you to your skis to help you carve beautiful turns, take sweet jumps, and dodge the odd out-of-control beginner.

To get the boot's shape right, an oven melts rough thermoplastic chips and pumps the liquid plastic into metal molds. The molds clamp together with a force of over 2,200 pounds. That's like having a rhinoceros on your toe! Then the molds pop open and robotic arms pull out the brand-new boot shells.

An assembler **rivets** rubber protectors to the soles so you don't slip while heading to the lodge for your cup of cocoa. Other workers rivet buckles on and add some plastic cuffs. They put radar reflectors in some models too, to help rescuers find you if you're caught in an avalanche. Then they attach long straps that help adjust the fit.

Now it's time for toasty liners. A machine cuts shapes from sheets of insulating fabric. Workers sew the pieces together and glue on warming layers made of polyurethane and polyester. Another machine squeezes the layers together into a kind of warming "sock" that will fit around your foot.

Workers stitch the seams and add waterproofing fabric with a special weave that keeps your feet from slipping around inside. Mechanical arms hold the boots open while an assembler slides the liners in.

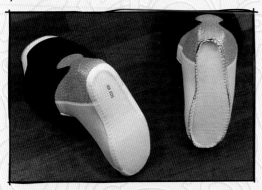

It only takes about an hour to make these boots. Then they're ready for the bumps, groomers, steeps, and deeps. Hot soup and sandwiches are extra.

Backcountry

Some special ski boots have rubber soles for hiking. Backcountry skiers don't use ski lifts. Instead, they hike up without their skis on, or leave the skis on and stick synthetic animal skins to the bottoms. The bristles in the "skins" let them walk straight up a steep slope before stripping the skins off and shredding the pristine powder.

Avalanche!

An avalanche happens when a weak layer of snow under the surface suddenly lets go. An entire mountainside can start sliding all at once, shattering into snow boulders as big as the family car. At the bottom of the slope, the moving snow sets up as hard as concrete. If you're ever in an avalanche, try to stay above it, so you don't end up inside a rock-hard mountain of fresh ice.

WORDS TO KNOW

Rivet: To attach two items with a gun that shoots a metal fastener through both.

FISHING LINE

Strong Strand

Early fishing lines were made from vines, cloth, and even horsehair. Today, fishermen use braided **synthetics** to haul in bass or pike. Stronger than steel, these lines won't snap if you hook the big one!

The line in this picture is made of a tough synthetic called ultra-high molecular-weight polyethylene. Say that five times fast. You've seen this special kind of plastic before in milk jugs and water pipes, and it's also used in bulletproof vests. It's super strong.

To make the line, a worker pulls the ends of fibers from big spools. She threads the ends through needles and spring-loaded parts in a machine called a maypole braider. It's called that because its spools spin and move like dancers around a maypole.

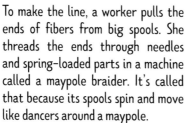

As they spin, the spools weave the strands into a braid. Incredibly, this factory has 4,500 braiding machines. They spin fast, but making a tight braid takes time. They'll spend seven to ten days to braid one 2,300-meter length of fishing line. Big spools overhead spin slowly, taking up the freshly braided line. The spools get loaded into a giant pressurized tank to dye the new line yellow.

After a load test, an automated system winds the line onto smaller spools of 137 meters each. A worker snips the ends, sticks on a label, and puts each spool in a cardboard box. It's strong and slender, making it easy to cast and reel—until you hook the one that got away!

The woven lines after being pressurized with the yellow dye!

Not dino-line

The plastic in your fishing line was created from synthetic fibers, made by processing petroleum. That's fossil fuel! Although it's fun to think of it as mashed-up dinosaurs, it's mostly the remains of ancient marine bacteria and algae.

No small fry

The biggest fish ever caught was a 2,664-pound great white shark. That's about the weight of a compact SUV, and trust us—you'd rather be inside the SUV!

WORDS TO KNOW

Synthetics: Manufactured fibers made from chemicals.

SCIENCE & TECHNOLOGY

Science is the study of the world around us. It's the way we tackle questions about our bodies, our environment, and everything else—from how massive galaxies form to what's inside the microscopic atom. Technology is a little different. It uses science to try to make our world a better place. It's the way we solve problems, like how to get drinking water when there's no stream or lake nearby, or how to see the farthest star or send a robot car to Mars. The inventions in this section help us clean our floors, light up our nights, and even print with solid metal.

LAPTOPS

Electronic Wonders

The first computers were massive—the size of an entire room. Good luck getting your homework done on that! Thankfully, scientists spent more than 70 years hatching thousands of ideas to make them faster, smaller, and more powerful. Today, the ultra-powerful gaming laptop you see being built in these pages is 400,000 times faster than its early ancestors—and 120,000 times lighter. But have you ever wondered how factories make these magical machines?

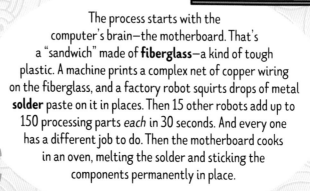

The process starts with the computer's brain—the motherboard. That's a "sandwich" made of **fiberglass**—a kind of tough plastic. A machine prints a complex net of copper wiring on the fiberglass, and a factory robot squirts drops of metal **solder** paste on it in places. Then 15 other robots add up to 150 processing parts *each* in 30 seconds. And every one has a different job to do. Then the motherboard cooks in an oven, melting the solder and sticking the components permanently in place.

The laptop's bottom half comes next. Assemblers add speakers to let gamers hear the zaps and roars as they fight monsters, aliens, and other other nasties. Then a computer-guided saw cuts holes for two huge cooling fans. Gaming laptops make a lot of heat, and need big fans to keep your knees from getting scorched.

Once the motherboard is cool, a team of workers adds a fifteen-inch liquid crystal display screen **(LCD)**. They snap in a microphone and webcam and screw on two hinges that connect the laptop's halves. They plug in a **Wi-Fi** antenna too, so you can surf the web or send a skiing video to grandma.

Then the workers screw in the motherboard, cleaning its delicate connections with compressed air and a chemical cleaner called solvent. Then comes the solid-state drive (**SSD**) that stores games, information, and maybe even the odd homework assignment. They also add a high-capacity battery to let you battle baddies for hours without a power cord.

How do they make computer chips?

The computer's processor and hard drive are made of tiny chips of a unique material called semiconductors. To make them, factories melt silicon—the main ingredient in beach sand and quartz crystals. Workers cool the silicon and slice it into wafers, and engineers "print" complex wiring patterns on them with a process like photography. Up to thirty layers of printed circuitry may stack up to make a single chip.

Last, they add the keyboard and run a full range of tests. The coolest thing about this laptop? In a few years, the factory will make them even faster, smaller, and more powerful. By the time you've graduated college, your computer will make this one look like an antique!

Fiberglass: A material made of spun glass fibers and glue-like resin. To make it, glass is heated, melted, and pushed through tiny holes to make fibers. These fibers then get coated with resin-glue to stick them together into a hard sheet.

LCD: Liquid crystal display. A computer screen that squeezes millions of tiny plastic-like crystals between glass or plastic sheets. When a light shines through them, each crystal lets through a different mix of red, green, and blue to make a picture.

Semiconductor: A material that can both conduct electricity and insulate against it. Prized in making computers because it's easy to control how much it conducts. That control helps computers "think."

Solder: To join two metal parts together, usually by melting a solder paste made of a mix of lead and tin.

SSD: Solid-state drive. A stack of silicon computer chips that store information even when the power's off. Tiny bits of electricity called electrons get "trapped" inside the chips in a special way that forms a movie, game, or picture of your family dog.

Wi-Fi: A trade name for a networking technology that sends encoded messages through the air as radio waves.

3-D METAL PRINTERS

Solid Machines

"Hey mom, can I print a motorcycle?" We can't do that yet, but 3-D metal printers *can* print all sorts of complex metal parts for complicated machines. Imagine printing a part to fix a spaceship while you're up in space, or a replacement part for the family car while you're sitting in your living room.

A 3-D metal printer works by firing a laser to melt a special metal powder into liquid. A cone-shaped nozzle squirts a thin stream of this hot metal in a pattern controlled by a computer. It adds layer after layer, kind of like making a glue sculpture, but with a lot more finesse. When the goo cools, you've got a shiny metal part. The part you see here is a heat exchanger for a rocket nozzle.

To make the printer, technicians start by designing the print head on a computer. It takes hundreds of hours to create the full design. When the planning work is finished, computer-guided tools carve the nozzle cone from a bar of brass. Other tools carve out a shiny part that will eventually feed metal powder to the nozzle. They cut little tunnels in it for the different metal powders it will use.

A worker screws on a channel for the laser. She adds latches to make the whole part easy to take apart later for cleaning, and she screws on another nozzle to guide the laser. Next she fastens on a metal cover for safety. The whole part now looks kind of like a space rocket.

Another worker mounts a laser system to a printer box. He adds tubes for coolant and screws the printer head in place.

Next, they make the feeder. That's a part that pushes metal powder to the nozzle. They connect shafts and **cylinders**, and screw on a spinning disc to move the powder through the system. A worker adds a small gas jet to help it flow. He screws round windows to the lid too, so we can see the powder swirl inside. No secrets here!

He adds a cone to feed the metal powder, and the clear plastic tube that holds it, called a **hopper**. He clamps the feeder motor to the top with long screws and mounts the whole thing to the printer box. Now we're ready to print metal parts like magic. Printed motorcycle—here we come!

What can 3-D printers make?

Metal printers can make complex gears, brackets, turbines, tubes, and nozzles. Other types of 3-D printers have made guitars, flutes, medical models, phone cases, clocks, bikes, and even robot birds and houses! A 3-D printer can make intricate devices too—like a ball of different-colored, interlocking, moving gears, all in a single print.

WORDS TO KNOW

Cylinder: A three-dimensional shape like a tall circle. Examples of cylinders are food cans, posts, and layer cakes.

Hopper: A container used to feed free-flowing material like powder, sand, rice, or coal, usually by gravity. It's often shaped like a cone to prevent clogging.

VACUUM CLEANERS

Dirt Destroyers

What would we do without vacuum cleaners? These time-saving miracles can clean our floors in minutes. That can get you outside playing fast—instead of inside doing chores for hours. But the first vacuum cleaner was so big, it had to be dragged from place to place by horses!

The vacuum cleaner in your house works with an electric motor that spins a fan to suck up dirt. To build the motor in this sleek little canister model, a robot starts with a round part called a **rotor** and adds two white plastic discs. The discs will **insulate** the rotor, stopping its electricity from "leaking out." The rotor itself will spin inside another part, turning electricity into mechanical motion to spin the vacuum cleaner's fan.

A second robot adds a round copper part called a commutator. It will act as a switch, controlling the motor's electric current. A machine wraps thin wire around the newly assembled part hundreds of times. The coil of wire will turn the rotor into an electromagnet that will make the motor spin.

Another robot welds the commutator to the wires. A machine adds a cover to the rotor assembly to keep the vacuum cleaner quiet while the rotor spins. Next, spouts drip liquid plastic resin on the coil of wires to keep them tight. Then a robot shaves a little metal off the commutator to smooth it out. During this whole process, machines test different parts of the rotor several times.

The worker adds a carbon brush to make electrical contact with the rotor inside the stator.

More robots add parts called bearings that will connect the rotor to the rest of the vacuum cleaner. Then they put the rotor in a plastic box called a housing. Inside the housing sits a special part called a **stator**. Electricity will move through it, making the magnetic rotor spin, and moving the fan blades to suck up those dust bunnies.

A worker adds more parts that help the motor work, including a carbon brush, a diffuser shield, and an impeller plate to keep things cool.

DID YOU KNOW?

Did you know some of the dirt in your house is so small you can't even see it? It's made of nasties like mold, pollen, and bacteria. To keep it from blowing back into the air where you could breathe it in—Achoo!—a worker tucks a filter into a special slot. He snaps on a cover packed with brush attachments, and the vacuum cleaner is ready to clean up your life.

So far, we don't have anything that looks like a vacuum cleaner. We've just been building a highly efficient motor that looks like a sort of pill made out of metal and white plastic. Now it's time to add the part that holds the fan blades. A machine checks that part by spinning it, cutting weight off here or there until it's perfect.

Now we're ready to put the motor and fan assembly into the vacuum cleaner body. The motor is shipped to another factory, where a **technician** adds a rubber seal to the bottom part of the vacuum cleaner's housing, and adds the reel that holds the power cord in place. He adds the fan and motor assembly too, and snaps on a back panel.

The dust bag being added to the frame of the cleaner body.

You wouldn't be able to suck up sand after a trip to the beach without a power switch. So an **assembler** screws on a panel with an on/off switch and other controls. He adds a rubber bumper to keep your walls from getting bruised, and a bag to catch the dirt. Then robots connect the frame and housing, and a worker adds the foot switch that retracts the power cord.

How does an electric motor work?

You've felt the power of a magnet. That same power is the simple force that makes electric motors work. In the motor sits an electric magnet made of a spool of copper wire, called a rotor. The wire sits in a piece of metal, called a stator, but the metal in the rotor and the stator never touch. When you turn the power on, the current in the magnet changes. As the magnet tries to "flip" to its natural position, it spins a shaft, powering a toy robot, electric car, or household vacuum cleaner.

WORDS TO KNOW

Assembler: A human worker who puts parts of a machine together in a factory. (See: *technician*)

Insulate: To keep electricity or heat from moving from one place to another.

Rotor: The spinning part in an electric motor, wound with hundreds of loops of copper wire.

Stator: A metal part that sits around a rotor in an electric motor.

Technician: An employee in a factory who puts together the different parts of a machine. (See: *assembler*)

SOLAR PANELS

Power from the Sun

The sun is the source of all the energy in our solar system. Not so long ago, the idea of harvesting that energy seemed like something from a science fiction book. Today, nonpolluting solar power is practical and economical, and the future of solar panels is blindingly bright.

To make a solar panel, technicians connect thirty-six hard plates of silicon called modules to form a full panel. The modules are flat "collectors" that change sunlight into electricity—also called **photovoltaic cells**. The technicians add a welding cleaner called **flux** to the connections. It's there to clean the metal and make the liquid solder stick in place. Then they use a soldering iron to connect a wire to each module. Once everything's connected, they clean the modules with **ultrasound** waves in a warm water bath.

They add more flux and put nine modules together in a group, joining four groups to make a panel. They handle the modules with suction grips because they're so thin, you could easily break one with your hands.

The workers solder all thirty-six modules to a metal strip. The strip will funnel the electricity from all the modules to a single place.

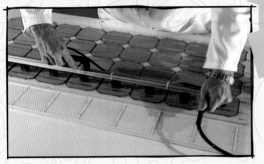

How do they make a photovoltaic cell?

Just like a computer chip, a photovoltaic cell is a thin slice of silicon with wiring running through it. Each cell starts with pure silicon—the main ingredient in beach sand and quartz crystals. It's treated with chemicals, melted, and sliced into square sheets. These go into a metal frame and get a coating of protective silicon film.

Now they put the modules on a sheet of glass. They stick them to the glass with sealing film—like a giant sticker. They put the whole thing in an oven, suck out all the air, and bake it. When it's done, they test it in a solar simulator, shining a bright light on it to see how much electricity it makes. It takes about an hour to make a solar panel like this. Hold the sunscreen, please.

WORDS TO KNOW

Flux: A liquid or paste used to prepare materials for soldering. It seals out air, cleans the material, and attracts the metal solder, making it "stick" better.

Photovoltaic cells: Also known as solar cells, photovoltaic cells are electronic components that convert the sun's light into electricity.

Ultrasound: High-frequency sound waves too high-pitched for the human ear. They can be used to "see" inside people or objects, and to vibrate dirt and contaminants from materials.

ALKALINE BATTERIES

Portable Energy

When you use a walkie-talkie, TV remote, or remote-controlled car, you use alkaline batteries. These little tubes of electricity make our lives work better, from shining a flashlight beam into a spooky cave to juicing up your favorite laser sword. But are they magic? Nope. They're chemistry.

The alkaline batteries you see here are the rechargeable type that last for years. To start making them, the factory cuts nickel-plated steel into small oval pieces. The factory workers shape each piece into a tube, and fill it with important chemical ingredients:

- *Graphite* to conduct electricity.
- *Silver catalyst* to prevent pressure buildup.
- *Manganese dioxide* to bind the ingredients in one half of the battery.
- *Zinc* to bind the ingredients in the other half.
- *A gelling agent* to keep the zinc particles suspended.
- *Potassium hydroxide* to work as an *electrolyte* to make electricity.

Each battery has two halves: an **anode** and a **cathode**. Electricity will flow from the anode into a device like a flashlight and then back into the battery's cathode. The cathode contains a special mix of chemicals and materials. A twenty-five-head press shapes the cathode's chemicals into hollow pellets. It makes twenty-five thousand pellets every hour. Then a machine puts three pellets inside each battery. Why three? Because the pellets are delicate, and it's easier to handle three smaller ones without breaking any than trying it with one big one. Then a machine seals one end of the battery.

Next, the workers cut a roll of paper into little strips. The strips have microscopic holes to let ions flow through. Ions are electrically charged molecules.

A hot-glue machine rolls and glues the strips into a tube shape, and another machine puts them in the batteries. Then each battery gets a squirt of liquid called an electrolyte that soaks through the paper and fills the hollow pellets. Next comes a squirt of zinc gel, and a top secret chemical that makes the batteries rechargeable.

Another machine tests each one for a fraction of a second, making sure it has the right amount of **volts**. A labeling machine adds a plastic label. Then three seconds in an oven shrinks the label to make a tight fit. Okay, where's your electric toothbrush?

DID YOU KNOW?

Did you know there's a nail inside each battery? It's where the electricity collects when you're not using it. A welding machine fuses these nails onto the bottoms of the battery caps. Then a machine puts on the caps. Each one gets a safety feature crucial to rechargeable batteries—a tiny vent in case of pressure buildup. Without that vent, the battery could explode! Then the machine closes up each battery.

The finished batteries, labeled, packaged and ready to energize!

75

MAKE A POTATO BATTERY

You will need:
- 6 alligator clips
- 3 copper wires about 8 inches long
- 2 copper nails
- 2 big potatoes, thoroughly washed
- 2 galvanized nails
- A battery-powered clock that runs on one AAA battery.

1. Connect the alligator clips to the ends of the copper wire.
2. Push a galvanized nail into one end of each potato.
3. Push a copper nail into the other end of each potato.
4. Using the wires, connect the galvanized nail of the first potato to the copper nail of the second.
5. Connect the copper nail of the first potato to the galvanized nail of the second.
6. Connect the copper nail of the first potato to the positive (+) terminal in the battery case of the clock.
7. Connect the galvanized nail of the second potato to the negative (–) terminal of the clock.

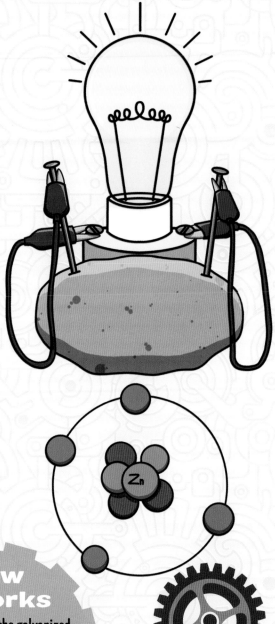

How it works

The zinc ions in the galvanized nails travel through the wires to react with the copper ions in the copper nails. The moving ions make the clock work. The acid in the potatoes works as an electrolyte.

How do batteries make electricity?

A battery makes an electrical current when its positive end—the cathode—and its negative end—the anode—connect through a "helper" substance called an electrolyte. This pathway makes the battery strip electrons from its chemicals, sending them down the wires into your flashlight bulb.

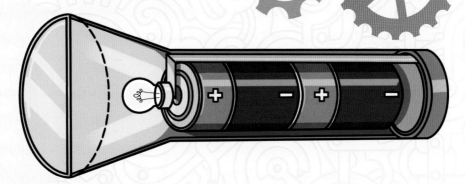

WORDS TO KNOW

Anode: The "negative" end of an alkaline battery. Electrons flow out of the anode and into an electrically powered device, such as a flashlight.

Cathode: The "positive" end of an alkaline battery. Electrons flow from the anode into an electrically powered device and then back into the battery through the cathode.

Volts: A way to measure the power of an electric current, just like we use *pounds* to measure weight or *miles per hour* (or *kilometers per hour*) to measure speed. Volts measure the electric potential of a specific place in an electric circuit.

MOTION SENSORS

Moving Pictures

Have you ever wondered how a smartphone knows to rotate a picture of a map or compass when you turn it? It's because a tiny motion sensor inside the phone—called an accelerometer—knows which way is up . . . or left or right. The sensor is a silicon chip with circuitry so small you'd need a microscope to see it.

Each chip starts with melted silicon. It's cooled and sliced to make thin discs called wafers. A technician puts them in a rack and then into a heat-resistant carrier made of quartz.

How do motion sensors work?

The most common type of motion sensor uses tiny crystals that store electric charges every time they move. The printed circuitry can analyze these charges to learn which way the phone is moving or tilting, and how fast.

The carrier goes into a 2,000°F furnace. That's hot enough to melt the candles on your birthday cake and melt the baking sheet as well. Inside the furnace, heat and steam coat the wafers with a metal called an **oxide**. Then a machine adds a thin layer of aluminum so they'll conduct electricity.

The next part is like photography. Each wafer gets washed with a chemical that's sensitive to light. Then a bright **ultraviolet light** shines through a glass plate with a picture on it. The picture is a map of all the wiring used for thousands of motion sensors. The light burns the image of the wiring onto the wafers. Another chemical completes the process. It's like making an old-style photograph. Say cheese!

To separate the wafer into all those motion sensors, a robot shoots it with a stream of gas called **plasma**. That breaks the wafer's surface into thousands of free-moving 3-D motion sensors. Then a sprayer cleans them with a blast of gas.

A robot flips the wafer like a pancake, puts it in a clamping system, and stacks another wafer on the top. Then another machine heat-seals them together. *Sss!* A computerized saw cuts grooves in the top wafer, while a stream of water keeps the dust down. The saw uncovers the thin layer of aluminum to let the wafer layers make electrical connections.

It takes three weeks to turn a wafer into thousands of motion-sensing chips. Each one gets cut from the wafer, encased in plastic, and tested. Then a robot packages them for shipping. Now no matter which way you turn, you'll always know which way is up.

WORDS TO KNOW

Accelerometer: A motion sensor, often in a smartphone or tablet.

Oxide: A chemical compound made of oxygen and other elements. The rust on the bottom of a car is an oxide, but so is the shiny coating on the aluminum foil in your kitchen.

Plasma: An energized gas used in cutting torches. You see a giant ball of plasma in the sky almost every day. It's the sun!

Ultraviolet light: Invisible radiation that causes summer tans and sunburns. It's used for "burning" images on silicon computer chips.

URANIUM

Power from Below

Nuclear power plants make a lot of the electricity that lights our homes. Their energy comes from uranium—a heavy metal first discovered more than two hundred years ago. No one knew it was important until 1938, when scientists learned to split its atoms, unleashing the tremendous energy inside.

The nuclear fuel bundle you see here is as big as a fireplace log, but it contains as much energy as 71,000 gallons of oil. But turn off the lights before you leave the room anyway, okay? Because it's really hard to make.

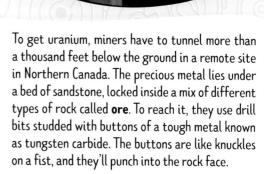

To get uranium, miners have to tunnel more than a thousand feet below the ground in a remote site in Northern Canada. The precious metal lies under a bed of sandstone, locked inside a mix of different types of rock called **ore**. To reach it, they use drill bits studded with buttons of a tough metal known as tungsten carbide. The buttons are like knuckles on a fist, and they'll punch into the rock face.

During mining, the ore could collapse and kill the miners, so they have to freeze it first, to keep it safely in place. To freeze the ore, a mining machine drills 426 feet from the mine tunnel into the sandstone bed. It takes eight days to connect just one of the many five-foot pipes they'll need. When they're done, a cooling machine above ground chills a chemical called calcium bromide to -22°F. The chemical flows down the pipes, freezes the ore, and loops back up top to get chilled again. Don't stick your tongue to this flagpole! The freezing process also turns underground water into ice. Without that step, the water could flood the mine.

Next, workers in a tunnel above the ore deposit use a three-headed drill to make a long, skinny hole, called a **pilot hole**. The hole pokes down through the ore and into a big tunnel the miners make underneath. In that lower tunnel, miners attach a large bit called a **reamer** to the drill. It's covered with button-encrusted wheel-tentacles. The miners pull this bit up through the pilot hole to widen it, and the broken ore falls down the shaft and fills the room below.

Now a remote-control tram scoops up the rock. Using remote machinery lets the miners keep far away from falling rocks and radiation. After the tram scoops up the ore, it dumps it down a chute. Meanwhile, another worker sits in a control room, using a remote hydraulic hammer to smash the ore to bits. These bits move to a mill that grinds them into sand. Mixing it with water, technicians pump it to the surface, where they truck it to a mill.

The mill uses vacuum pumps to suck up the wet ore mix—called **slurry**—into holding tanks. Slurp! Workers add acid to dissolve the uranium. The rock doesn't dissolve, so it drops to the bottom of the tanks and gets left behind. More chemical reactions purify the uranium. Then they roast it at 1,562°F, turning it into a jet-black powder.

The uranium moves through two more factories that process it with chemicals. Giant **centrifuges** spin it fast to mix it, and a pressing machine forms it into heavy pellets. Those harden and shrink inside another oven, and robots load them into tubes made of a heat-resistant metal called **zirconium**.

More robots weld caps onto the ends of these tubes, and load thirty-seven of them into a cylindrical rack. Then they weigh them, pack, and ship them. The fuel bundles are safe to handle now—until they're plugged into a nuclear reactor. Then they'll give off enough heat to light your nights for years to come.

Heavy metal

Uranium has an atomic number of 92. That means its atoms have 92 protons and usually the same number of electrons, depending on how many neutrons it has.

Powerful mineral

Just one fuel bundle of uranium contains the same amount of energy as 71,000 gallons of oil.

MAKE YOUR OWN URANIUM

No. You can't make your own uranium.

DID YOU KNOW?

Uranium takes its name from the planet Uranus.

How does nuclear power work?

In the core of a nuclear reactor, several fuel bundles are grouped together to form a fuel assembly. They're kept underwater to keep them cool. To make electricity, engineers lower the rods into the reactor core. With the fuel rods close together, neutrons begin to escape from the center of the uranium atoms—called the nuclei. When a zinging neutron hits a uranium atom, it splits it into two lighter atoms. This releases more neutrons, which split more atoms, creating a chain reaction and releasing massive amounts of heat. That warms up a water tank, turning water into steam that spins a turbine. A magnet attached to the turbine generates electricity.

WORDS TO KNOW

Centrifuge: A machine that spins material at high speeds to force contents of different weights to separate.

Ore: The raw, rough rock that contains a metal or other valuable mineral.

Pilot hole: A small hole drilled to guide a drill bit that makes a larger hole.

Reamer: A large drill bit that widens a smaller hole.

Slurry: A mix of liquids and solids that can be pumped from one place to another.

Zirconium: A silver-gray metal, highly resistant to heat and corrosion.

COMMERCIAL DRONES

Fly by Wire

A commercial drone is a small, unmanned aircraft with a camera. It can snag a bird's-eye view to help people plan roads or bridges, grow fruits and vegetables, or keep an eye on lakes and rivers. About five feet across, the drone shown here is called an octocopter. Just like an octopus has eight tentacles, this drone has eight propellers to keep it flying high. A computer "brain" inside the drone will slow some of the propellers and speed others up to make it turn or dip.

The drone's parts are made of **carbon fiber**—a hard, strong, light material. A computer-guided mill cuts out the legs and frames, and a technician sands their edges smooth.

A 3-D printer makes the sockets for the drone's propellers—known as **rotors**. Layer after layer, it squirts out a thin stream of liquid plastic that hardens to create the part. Then a technician adds a backing and a lever that will clamp the rotor arm in place. The tech connects an electronic speed controller, then screws the socket to the frame. Paper airplanes, eat your heart out!

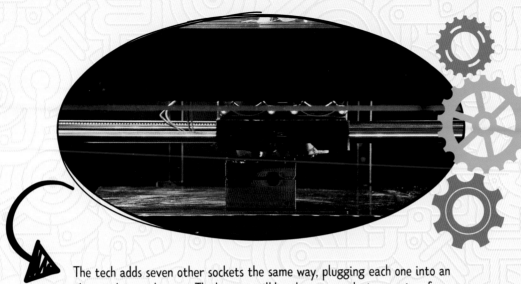

The tech adds seven other sockets the same way, plugging each one into an electrical power harness. The harness will let the rotors take instructions from an onboard computer called an autopilot.

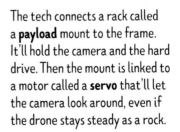

Help from above

In remote areas like Africa, drones deliver life-saving medicines and medical equipment to places where ground transport takes too long.

The tech connects a rack called a **payload** mount to the frame. It'll hold the camera and the hard drive. Then the mount is linked to a motor called a **servo** that'll let the camera look around, even if the drone stays steady as a rock.

Other workers use a machine called a **vacuum former** to shape a plastic cover for the drone's top. It heats a sheet of plastic, softening it. Then it sucks out air to pull the plastic tight against a wooden mold. When it cools, the workers trim the excess, cut a hole for the payload mount, and attach it to the frame.

The workers dropping the heated plastic onto the wooden mold!

Finally, they install the autopilot and the arms—eight carbon fiber tubes with plastic rotors driven by small motors. A pilot can drive the drone remotely, but she'll usually program it with **GPS** coordinates before takeoff. Up, up, and away!

Eye in the sky

Farmers use drones to see their crops. Insurance companies use them to see building damage after hurricanes, saving thousands of hours of legwork.

WORDS TO KNOW

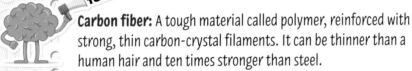

Carbon fiber: A tough material called polymer, reinforced with strong, thin carbon-crystal filaments. It can be thinner than a human hair and ten times stronger than steel.

GPS: Global Positioning System. A navigation system that uses radio signals from satellites to find an object's location.

Rotors: Spinning propellers, usually pointing up, used to provide the lift that makes a drone or helicopter fly.

Payload: The cargo that a vehicle is built to carry. Literally, the load that makes it pay.

Servo: A small motor in a machine. There are servos in your car's automatic windows, robot vacuum cleaners, and moving toys.

MUSIC

The oldest known musical instruments are from about forty thousand years ago but music has probably been around since the first birds showed up sixty million years ago. Today, your smartphone, tablet, or home voice assistant pump out sounds that would blow Mozart's hair back. Some instruments have changed a lot—like electric guitars—while some, like clarinets and saxophones, have hardly changed at all. But where do all the gadgets, gizmos, and instruments we use to "soothe the savage beast" come from? Let's take a look at a few musical inventions, and how they're made.

CLARINETS

Versatile Woodwinds

The word *clarinet* means "little trumpet." But, like saxophones, clarinets are called woodwinds because they make sound by vibrating a cane reed against the mouthpiece. The first one in history had only two finger keys, but more were added later to let musicians play a Mozart-worthy range of sounds.

The clarinet's keys are made of brass or nickel silver. Artisans make wax copies of the keys by squirting hot wax into key-shaped plaster molds. They stick lots of these copies onto a stem, gluing them on with more hot wax. This makes a funny-looking tree, and all its branches are wax keys. They put this tree into a cylinder, and then into a machine that fills the cylinder with a special silica-based liquid. The liquid hardens, forming a ceramic, and they melt the wax to leave behind a tree-shaped cavity called a mold.

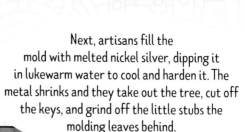

Next, artisans fill the mold with melted nickel silver, dipping it in lukewarm water to cool and harden it. The metal shrinks and they take out the tree, cut off the keys, and grind off the little stubs the molding leaves behind.

Now artisans want to coat the keys with silver. They do that with a process known as **plating**. The problem? Pure silver won't stick to a nickel silver alloy. So they polish the keys in a tumbler filled with synthetic stones, then submerge them in a chemical. They pass an electric current through the keys and throw some chunks of copper into the tank. Like a magnet, this process sticks tiny particles of metal to the keys until they've got a dressy silver coat.

Newly drilled tone holes in the plastic body!

A computerized drill bores twenty-four tone holes in a two-part plastic body, and forty smaller holes to hold the key posts. A machine presses posts into the smaller holes, zapping them with ultrasound to melt the plastic and stick the posts in place.

The next machine drills holes for rods that operate the keys. Artisans install the keys, each with a foam pad to keep air from leaking out. A musician puts the clarinet together and checks the movement. Then she adds the bell and mouthpiece. Handel or Benny Goodman, this clarinet is ready for the airwaves.

WORDS TO KNOW

Plate: To coat a metal object with a thin layer of a different and usually more valuable metal.

SAXOPHONES

Moody Horns

Have you ever wondered how the saxophone can sound so soft and sad sometimes, and yet so loud and happy others? It's the misty background of the saddest city street or the joyous romp of a New Orleans festival. The instrument was invented by Adolphe Saxe in the mid-1800s. He wondered, How can I mix the power of a brass horn with the emotion of a woodwind? His creation can sound either bright and edgy or dark and moody—a rare combination in a wind instrument.

Each saxophone starts out with a simple sheet of brass or copper. A hydraulic punch cuts it into rectangles, and a worker draws a pattern on each one. Another punch cuts out a cone-shaped piece, and the worker pounds it with a wooden stick to bend it.

More workers weld the seam, and hammer one end into a bell by hand. The hand-hammering changes the metal so it sounds more resonant.

Music Music Music

A craftsman slides the bell onto a form and brushes it with lubricant. The form spins against a roller, smoothing out dents and creating the familiar horn shape. Another worker uses a punch machine to cut the **tone holes**. Those will shape the sound, to help the sax play anything from Tchaikovsky to Lady Gaga.

The main body starts with a flat metal wedge. The craftspeople fold it, weld the seam, and cut more tone holes. They heat the holes, then slide the tube onto a steel form called a mandrel. Then they set a long guide rack on the tube, with lots of holes in it, feed tools into the holes, and pull the mandrel's rounded inserts up and through the tube. This bends the edges of the holes into a raised rim that will fit the **key cups**. The worker drills the rims to smooth and level them, so they don't sound like an angry emu when you play.

The punch machine in action!

The next part is the U-shaped "bow" that links the bell and body. The craftsman brushes flux onto the ends to clean them, then solders them to make an airtight seal.

A standard saxophone has twenty-three tone holes, with a key cup to close each one. This factory assembles each cup and key by hand with silver solder. Some keys get assembled on a brass plate called a rib, which then gets soldered to the saxophone.

Other workers polish the parts with a buffing wheel to give the brass a mirror finish. They dip the saxophone parts in a chemical bath and use strong sound waves to shake off leftover dirt and grease. Last, they spray lacquer on the brass to prevent corrosion.

A technician attaches the rods, keys, and cups. They use a flashlight to look for leaks between the cup and tube. The light escapes through unwanted cracks, telling the technician if they need to tighten things a bit. Then they add the needle springs that let the keys spring back after you play a note, covering the tone hole up again when you're not using it.

Last, the technician fits the bell bow to the body with screws and a connecting ring. It takes about a month to craft a saxophone like this. You can't rush perfection, so if you're in a hurry . . . well you'll just have to wait.

The Music Man

Adolphe Saxe, the saxophone's inventor, also created the saxhorn, which inspired the flugelhorn and euphonium. Though the saxophone failed to catch on with orchestras, its flexibility has made it popular in chamber music, jazz, marching bands, rock and roll, and of course detective movies.

How do saxophones make music?

When a musician blows into a saxophone, a reed in the mouthpiece vibrates to make sound. To play the different notes, the player changes the length of the air column in the instrument by opening and closing the tone holes. You can work the same air column trick by filling a few glasses with different amounts of water, then tapping them with a fork.

WORDS TO KNOW

Key cups: Cups that cover the tone holes in a wind instrument completely, blocking off the flow of air when they are not in use.

Tone holes: The openings in the body of a wind instrument that change the sound produced when they are closed or opened.

Woodwind: A type of musical instrument that makes sound when a musician blows air over a reed in the mouthpiece or over a mouth hole. Examples are clarinets, flutes, and saxophones.

HEADPHONES

Sound Inventions

To rock out to your favorite song or watch a movie without bugging Mom or Dad, headphones are a blast. But before your headphones landed on your ears, workers in a factory used several machines and a lot of handiwork to make them.

To start making a set of headphones, a machine squirts hot plastic into a mold to make several plastic parts. Another wraps hair-thin copper wire around a metal cylinder. This makes an important part called a **voice coil** that lets the headphones "speak." How does it work? When your phone or tablet sends an electrical signal to the coil, it vibrates a thin sheet of plastic called a **diaphragm**. That vibration creates the sound waves that travel through the air and bump into your ears.

To make the diaphragm, workers heat a plastic **membrane** with a special machine and press it into the desired shape. The diaphragm is thicker in the middle, letting it make any kind of sound, from the high-pitched whine of a mosquito to the rumble of a rocket taking off. A technician trims the diaphragm and glues it to the voice coil. Then she puts the diaphragm and voice coil in a plastic shell.

The signals for your favorite song will travel down a pair of curved, stiff wires. The stiffness of those wires will let them hold their shape as they curve over your head, helping the headphones sit snugly in place. Workers snap the wires together, adding a connector for another wire to plug in a phone or laptop.

Workers add an adjustable head-piece, then connect the two halves of the speaker shell with an air-powered—or **pneumatic**—tool. They put the speaker in the shell, with plastic brackets to protect it, then screw everything in place, and solder on the speaker wires. Last comes a headband and a plastic grill. Now these bad boys are wired for sound, and ready for your favorite entertainment in a way that's music to your ears.

How does a speaker work?

A traditional audio speaker is made of three basic parts: a diaphragm, a magnet, and a voice coil. When current passes through the coil, it creates a magnetic field, pushing it away from the magnet, vibrating the diaphragm, and making sound waves travel through the air. Your voice works the same way, by vibrating the mucous membranes of your vocal cords.

WORDS TO KNOW

Diaphragm: A diaphragm is a thin, semiflexible membrane in an audio speaker that creates sound waves.

Membrane: A thin, flexible surface. Your eardrums are thin membranes made of connective tissue in your ear canal. Nerves send their signals to your brain.

Pneumatic: The use of compressed air or gas to move the parts of a machine. Pneumatics are used in brakes, musical instruments, and (ugh) dental drills.

Voice coil: A coil of copper wire attached to the cone of an audio speaker.

ELECTRIC GUITARS

About to Rock

The electric guitar dates back to the 1920s, but it wasn't made for heavy metal or for blistering guitar solos. The inventor just wanted to make a regular acoustic guitar louder. By the 1950s, the design had changed into the thin, curved block of wood we know today, and jammin' out had been invented.

Guitar bodies are made of poplar or maple wood. Those are light, flexible woods that can handle a full range of vibrations to make different sounds. Workers use a saw to cut a plank into two matching pieces of a precise width and thickness. They number the two boards so they'll end up in the same guitar. Mixing boards is a real no-no for the sound.

Damp wood bends, so workers dry the boards for two months in a heated room. They glue them together, but the glue rewets them, so it's back to the dryer for two more months. Hope they brought a book. When the wood is ready, a computer-guided cutter carves the body shape, and workers sand and trim the shape's rough edges so it's comfy when you're riffing out.

Workers make the neck by slicing a piece of hard-rock maple in half with a diamond-edged saw. They glue on a thin sheet of maple to the front of one half, then flip and glue it to the other. Flipping the wood grain strengthens the neck, to keep your ax from getting lax.

The body shape fully sanded, cleaned, and ready to be painted and glossed.

But uh-oh—over time, tight strings will start to bend the neck and wreck the sound. No problem. A computer-guided cutter shapes the neck and cuts a groove to hold a steel bar called a truss rod. The player can straighten it by twisting the rod.

When you play a guitar, you let your fingers do the walking down the **fingerboard**. That's the part you press to make the notes and chords. It's made of maple, ebony, or rosewood. The artisans glue it to the truss rod and use a vacuum press to make it stick.

Another automatic cutter finishes the neck's shape. A twenty-two-bladed saw cuts slots for the twenty-two **frets**—the metal lines on the fingerboard that shape the sound. A worker rounds and smooths the neck, then adds the wires.

99

If the frets aren't level, the guitar will buzz. Not a good sound! So workers color each one with a marker and wipe them with a sheet of sandpaper. Frets that are too high leave marker on the paper. Workers file these down, round them, and clean and protect the fingerboard with mineral oil. Now the neck looks good enough to eat!

The worker filing the frets down with a special curved file.

The workers add six tuning keys—one per string. These can be black or they can be gold or nickel plated. They add a thin piece of bone or plastic with grooves to hold the strings apart. It's called the nut. They check its height with a digital gauge because if it's not exactly right, we'll get that dreaded buzzing sound again.

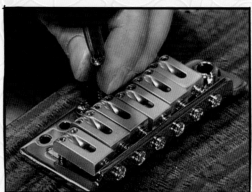

Another worker puts the guitar's body in a **silk-screen** printer to add the company name. Ultraviolet light dries the fresh ink. They apply sealant, then spray on twenty-two coats of stain and lacquer for a gorgeous, glossy finish. They dry it for six weeks, then sand and buff it to a mirror finish.

They join the neck and body with four bolts, then solder on control knobs for volume and tone. They also drill screw holes for the **bridge**. That's the bracket at the base of the guitar that holds the strings.

How do electric guitars work?

A magnet-and-coil assembly called a pickup works like a mini microphone. It picks up sound vibrations from the strings and sends them to an amplifier speaker that sends out that trademark electric guitar sound.

The volume and tone knobs come next, tucked into a cavity in back. Then comes a pickup selector switch and a jack for the guitar cord. They plug in the cable, test the pickups, add the strings, and presto. It's into a soundproof booth for a rockin' test drive. AC/DC, anyone?

Best of both

This guitar has an extra pickup near the neck's base that lets it sound both acoustic and electric.

WORDS TO KNOW

Bridge: A short bracket at the base of a guitar's neck. It supports the strings, transmitting the vibration. All stringed instruments, including violins and cellos, have bridges.

Fingerboard: The face of a guitar's neck where the player's fingers press the strings to make a sound. Also called a fretboard.

Frets: Short metal wires that run across a guitar's fingerboard, helping the guitar make sound. The frets divide the guitar's neck into fixed sections that represent the different musical notes.

Silkscreen: A method of printing that uses ink and a fine mesh screen to transfer an image to a surface.

HAND-BUILT JUKEBOXES

Throwback Tune Stack

Today, a quick tap on a smartphone plays a song. But there's a special charm to an old-fashioned push-button jukebox with colored bubble tubes and real vinyl records. It's a great way to get your next pizza party going in style.

To make this beautiful handcrafted work of art, artisans start with the cabinet. They glue together five skinny, flexible sheets of wood, and bend them into the curved shape of the jukebox in a dome-shaped mold. They glue on a back panel, and clamp the sheets together with **hydraulic** rams for twenty-four hours. Coffee break! When the glue dries, they remove the cabinet from the mold.

The artisans assemble the jukebox's fancy front door in a bracket called a **jig**, drilling screw holes for eight shiny, chrome-plated knuckles. The knuckles hold the high, curved door together on the top and sides. Then they paint or stain the wood—depending on whether they want a natural or colored finish. As your uncool uncle says, almost ready to go, Daddy-O!

Each jukebox has four straight bubble tubes and four curved ones along the top and sides to make your party extra colorful and fun. To make them bubble, an artisan seals the bottom of each tube, then dumps in tiny silicon crystals. They add a liquid that turns to gas at low temperature. Then they heat-seal each tube's top with a white-hot blowtorch, and heat it while another worker slowly bends it around a metal curving form.

Where do the bubbles come from? There's a sneaky heating plate at the bottom of each tube. When it warms, the crystals jiggle the liquid, turning it to gas. Instant bubbles! They float to the top, cool down, and turn back into liquid. The tubes go into clear plastic covers, and another worker wires the box for sound.

A transparent front door lets you watch as the machine finds, pulls, and plays each vinyl record. Inside, a round basket with 70 record slots holds 140 songs. It won't replace your smartphone, but it looks a whole lot cooler at a dance party.

How does a jukebox play a song?

When you choose a song, computer software tells the basket to spin to your record. A lift arm grabs it and drops it on a turntable. A motor spins the table, and the needle drops to play the track. You wouldn't want to wear this baby on an armband, but boy does it look nice.

How does a needle play a record?

To make a record, a factory converts a song into a special map of grooves and valleys, then presses them onto a vinyl disc. The disc has a single, long, spiral groove with a jagged bottom. When the needle or "stylus" bumps along the groove, it sends electrical signals to the speakers. Those make the sounds you hear when you rock out to Beyoncé or The Weeknd.

WORDS TO KNOW

Jig: A bracket that holds a work in progress and guides tools to shape or alter it.

Hydraulic: A way to move a machine using a motor-driven cylinder or hose filled with compressed liquid, such as oil or water.

Turntable: A spinning round table, often with a rubberized top, that spins a vinyl disc inside a record player.

ART

We store words on paper, and images and sounds in digital form. But what about a feeling? That's not such an easy thing to preserve. When artists want to save a special feeling, they "store" it in their art. They paint, sculpt, and draw things to convey it, sometimes even turning their work into animation on a movie screen. That way, they can share their emotions with others, and even with people who live thousands of years later. But how do they create their paintings, sculptures, and animations? Let's uncover some of the ways artists create and how a factory transforms wax and other ingredients to help us make our own art!

DIGITAL PAINTINGS

Art Imitates Art

Digital painting mixes computer technology with hand-on-canvas painting. Some studios even offer it as a way to turn your family photos into beautiful paintings.

For this digital painting, the photographer will use a collage of photos from a single family. Some of the photos aren't available in digital form, so she'll scan those in. She adjusts all the photos with a digital pen and tablet to improve the quality. She lays them out in an eye-catching way, then blends their edges so they flow together seamlessly.

She uses different digital brushes to add "paint," blurring the hard lines of the different images to make them look like painted pictures. This takes hours. When she finishes, she sends her work off to a lab.

There, a worker tweaks the painting, balancing the brightness and the colors. He prints a test sample to see how it looks, examining it with a powerful magnifying glass to check for mistakes.

Now it's time to print a full-sized copy of the painting. He puts a large roll of canvas on a printer. The printer uses special inks called **archival pigments** that will last for centuries—much longer than regular printer ink. The print head moves very slowly so it doesn't smear the thick ink. A digital painting like this—about three feet high—takes five hours to print.

The ink must dry for seventy-two hours. Then the worker adds a coat of lacquer to protect it from ultraviolet rays or handling. When the lacquer is dry, workers pull the canvas tight on a stretcher frame, staple it, and cut the corners.

The artist brushes on a clear-drying gel to add the texture of brush marks. Then she adds acrylic paints in places, creating depth and shading to make the painting come alive. She signs the painting, frames it, and adds a certificate of authenticity. Then she sticks the studio's label on the back. She has now immortalized a family's precious moments, captured by the camera lens.

WORDS TO KNOW

Archival pigments: Paints used in a printmaking process. The result is an image that lasts for centuries.

LITHOGRAPHS

Ancient Artwork

You never know what'll happen when you try something new. A Bavarian playwright discovered lithography by accident when he couldn't find a piece of paper to write down his laundry list. He scribbled the list on a flat rock with a grease pencil, and something special happened. When he put ink on the stone and on the pencil marks and pushed the stone onto a piece of paper, he got a perfect copy of his list.

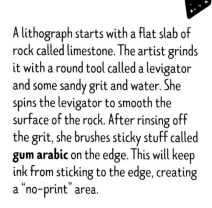

That may sound like small potatoes, but this was 1796 and there were no Wi-Fi printers yet. Before lithography, if you wanted to make a copy of a drawing, you had to write it with a pen. Before lithography, the playwright used to spend days making a set of copies of his scripts. After he discovered it, he was able to make copies for all the actors easily and quickly. We still use lithographs today because of their unique quality that gives art a special look.

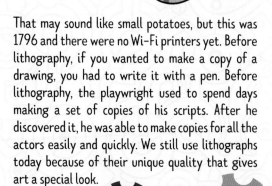

A lithograph starts with a flat slab of rock called limestone. The artist grinds it with a round tool called a levigator and some sandy grit and water. She spins the levigator to smooth the surface of the rock. After rinsing off the grit, she brushes sticky stuff called **gum arabic** on the edge. This will keep ink from sticking to the edge, creating a "no-print" area.

She marks up a blank piece of paper with a wax-and-charcoal crayon. Then she puts the paper on the stone, with the crayon facing down. She tapes a drawing over it, also facing down. Rembrandt, here we come!

She traces the drawing with a pencil, pressing hard. This transfers a backward image of the drawing to the stone. She peels the sheets of paper from the stone, then fills in the image with a greasy crayon, creating details like flecks of snow. Then she dusts the image on the stone with two powders called **rosin** and **talc**, then brushes on more gum arabic. These materials will protect the image and the stone from the acid etching liquid she'll brush on next—a mix of nitric acid and gum arabic. The **etching** liquid changes the stone's surface, making the image areas attract ink, while the nonimage areas will repel it.

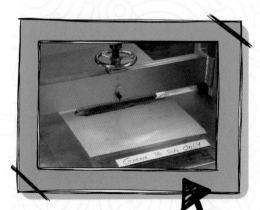

The paper being pressed on the scraper bar with the special lubricant oil.

She puts a fresh sheet of paper on the stone and spreads oil on two tools called a **scraper bar** and **tympan**. These will press the paper down hard onto the stone. She tightens the press, removes the tympan, and washes the stone. But something special has happened. A ghost image has been etched into the stone. She adds more oil onto the stone to create a base for the ink.

An assistant dampens the stone with a wet sponge. Then the artist rolls ink onto the stone with a big leather roller. The ink sticks to the greasy parts of the stone, but doesn't stick to the wet parts. She puts a sheet of print paper on top, puts a clear plastic tympan on the stone, and slides the stone beneath the scraper bar to print the image. When she lifts the paper, it shows a perfect copy of the drawing. Now she can make hundreds of the same print with the specially prepared stone. Each one is a work of art.

WORDS TO KNOW

Etching: Using acid to cut into a metal surface to create a design.

Gum arabic: A natural gum made of hardened sap from two types of acacia tree.

Rosin: A powder made from tree sap, used in lithography and violin playing.

Scraper bar: A bladed bar used to apply even pressure to transfer an image in lithography.

Talc: A clay mineral made of magnesium silicate. It's the chief ingredient in talcum powder.

Tympan: A thin plastic sheet that helps distribute pressure evenly in lithography.

MAKE YOUR OWN LITHOGRAPHY

You will need:
- Plastic gloves
- Heavy aluminum foil
- Tape
- A plastic cutting board or firm plastic sheet
- A writing instrument (grease pencil, permanent marker, colored pencil, ballpoint pen)
- A deep baking dish
- Cola
- Cooking oil
- Sponge
- Lithography ink
- A fine, small paint roller
- Paper ("rag paper" is best, but any kind will work)
- Cooking spoon

1. Wearing gloves to prevent fingerprints, cut a sheet of foil bigger than your drawing. Tape it tightly to a plastic sheet like a cutting board. Draw your picture—in reverse!—on the foil with your writing instrument.
2. Put the foil and plastic in a deep baking pan. Cover it with cola, making sure it clings to all the areas you didn't color. Then rinse it quickly with a wet sponge. The acid and gum arabic in the cola have begun to etch the foil.
3. Pour some cooking oil on the foil and wipe it gently with a soft cloth. A ghost of your drawing will take shape.
4. Wet the foil with a damp sponge.
5. Pour lithography ink on the foil, using the roller to spread it. The ink won't stick to the parts you didn't draw. Quickly wet the foil again with the damp sponge, picking up excess ink and rinsing it in the sink between wipes.
6. Press the paper on the freshly inked plate. You can wet the paper first to bring out fine details. Then rub the paper all over with the back of a large cooking spoon, and lift it up to see your print. Don't get discouraged if it doesn't work on your first try. Lithography takes practice!

GLASS
SCULPTURES

Clear Beauty

The ancient Egyptians were the first to make glass sculptures. You wouldn't want to play baseball around such a fragile work of art, but its ghostlike quality holds a special charm.

The artist who made the sculpture of a horse on this page combined two passions—love of horses and her art. The model for this statue was the artist's own horse. Her inspiration came from watching the swell of muscles as he romps, then shaping glass to re-create that same graceful feeling.

The artist started with some sketches of her horse in different stances. This is called an artistic study. It helps her settle on a form before she shapes the glass.

Next, she cleans rods of heat-resistant **borosilicate glass**. She softens them with a special blowtorch to fuse two of the rods, then sculpts the golden, glowing glass with tweezers and flat, knife-like tools until it starts to look like the horse's hips and legs. She has to work quickly so the glass won't cool and crack. She shapes a smaller piece of glass into a tail, turning her work constantly to see it from all angles.

The artist melts more glass to build the body and shape the horse's belly, back, and chest. This takes intense precision. She keeps the glass at exactly the right temperature with her well-adjusted blowtorch, and with constant motion.

She adds glass to the front and sculpts the shoulders and part of the front legs. While she works, she drops unwanted bits of sizzling glass in water to cool them so she won't get burned. Soft glass is almost 600°F!

Work stops while the unfinished piece goes into a kiln to bake. This is called a first **annealing**. It realigns the glass **molecules** so they won't crack.

The partially sculpted glass horse compared to the original drawing.

The head and mane come next. This is much more detailed work, so she uses smaller tools. She shapes the eye sockets first, then melts blobs of black glass into them, shaping them into eyes with a flat knife. She carves creases above them for the lids.

Now the artist adds glass for the ears and thins them with a squeezing tool called a **masher**. Oh, no! The ears get stuck together, so she cuts them apart again, then tweaks them on the horse's head using tweezers. Then she melts the head onto the body to create a seamless whole.

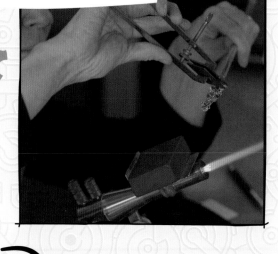

More melted glass creates a flowing mane. After another annealing, she finishes the legs, cutting off the tips and using black glass for the hooves.

This next part is critical. The hooves must end in a perfect angle or the horse could topple over and shatter. She uses tools to tweak each hoof until she's satisfied her horse will stand like a Kentucky Derby champion.

After a last annealing, the artist shines a polarized light through her work to check for stresses that could weaken it. She doesn't find any, and this galloping glass art is ready for a place of pride.

Melting glass

The next time you're out walking on the beach, look for rough, sand-colored rocks with bits of shells or smaller rocks inside. This is silica glass, made when lightning hits the beach and melts the sand! Some people call it petrified lightning.

WORDS TO KNOW

Annealing: Heating glass or metal, then letting it cool slowly to remove internal stresses.

Borosilicate glass: A special heat-resistant glass made from silica and a chemical called boron trioxide.

Masher: A squeezing tool for shaping glass or other materials during sculpting.

Molecules: The smallest piece of any element like iron, silicon, water, or sugar.

COPPER SCULPTURES

Tarnished Beauty

Artists have been working with copper for thousands of years. It's soft enough to cut, shape, and emboss. Left out in the weather, its bright and shiny surface tarnishes to create a warm spotted turquoise colored finish called a patina. The intricate copper sculptures on this page were made by a self-taught artist with a quirky imagination. Many of his works rotate on rods, as lawn art or weather vanes.

When a customer **commissions** a sculpture—or when inspiration strikes—he draws the art on thick, stiff paper called card stock. For a spinning sculpture like this gryphon, he draws the side view first. He cuts off extra paper with scissors, then uses smaller scissors to cut along the lines he drew. He lays the pattern on a sheet of a special thin copper.

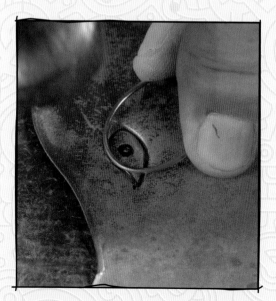

Now it's time to tape the pattern down and trace it with a fine-point pen. He repeats this on another sheet because the sculpture will have two sides. Then he cuts along the line with metal shears, trimming big pieces first and small ones second, just like when he cut the paper.

He draws an eye, then taps a hammer on a piece of wire to make the eyelid. He uses tools designed for stamping leather to shape the head. Working on the back of the metal sheet, he makes the details push out on the front.

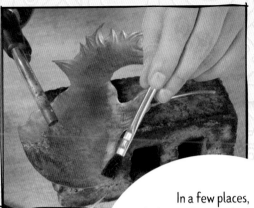

He heats the copper with a torch, adds flux to clean the edge, and melts some silver-based solder to the copper to create details. This is called pre-soldering, because he's not ready to connect the parts yet.

In a few places, he heats the metal to create a rainbow of colors. Then he melts the solder that he put on earlier to join the parts together. Where the sides are too far apart, he cuts a copper patch and uses it to bridge the gap.

The artist pre-soldering the back of the pieces with solder and heat.

A grinding tool flattens the seams. As a last step, he solders a ball bearing into a copper tube to let the weathervane spin. Then he solders the tube to the sculpture. Now this gorgeous gryphon weather vane is ready for your yard or barn roof.

Hammering

Artists use different tools for different effects. Hammering a malleable metal from the back to sculpt the front is called repoussé. It's French for "pushed back."

WORDS TO KNOW

Commission: A work order to create a piece of art or do a task.

Malleable: Workable or able to be shaped by hammering or pressing without breaking.

Patina: A sheen or glossy surface that comes from polishing, age, or corrosion.

ANIMATION

Moving Pictures

In the golden years of animation, teams of artists would draw dozens of pictures by hand for every second of finished film. Today, the process is done on a computer, but that doesn't mean it's any less artistic.

It all starts from a screenplay with dialogue and physical descriptions of the characters and scenery. The art director chooses what everything will look like. He draws mock-ups of the characters in pencil, tracing over them with a felt pen. He erases the pencil and adds shadows, then draws the backgrounds and the objects that will appear in them.

A **storyboard** artist comes in next. That's a special worker who tells the full story with a set of quick drawings. The production team will follow the storyboard the way you'd follow a recipe for lasagna in your kitchen. They enlarge the drawings, scan them into the computer, then play them in order. This kind of storytelling tool is called an **animatic.**

Meanwhile, animators bring the characters to life. They use special software to make a hidden skeleton inside each character. They move that framework with the software to make the body move. They add color, clothing, facial features, texture, and shadowing. A software tool moves mouths and lips to match the words said by each character. They work syllable by syllable, picking the mouth movement that matches each sound. It's a painstaking process that takes months to finish.

Another animator adds lighting effects. Then they cut and paste the characters and objects into the backgrounds, and program a **rough cut** of the show.

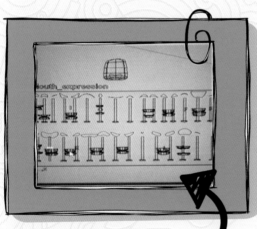

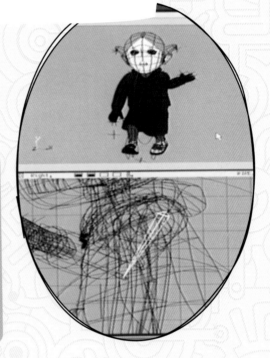

A selection of digital mouth expressions to match dialogue.

In the studio, the actors say their lines. A sound technician uses more computer software to mix the voices, music, and sound effects. They match the sounds to the rough cut, then refine the colors, textures, and movements. It takes a full year to make one half-hour film—and more than 42,000 drawings. Ouch! Our knuckles hurt just thinking about it.

Tech makes it better

Today, cutting-edge technology makes animation easier. New techniques let computers move a character's mouth by analyzing sound waves, then moving the lips, teeth, tongue, and face to match the voice.

WORDS TO KNOW

Animatic: A rough version of a movie or TV show, using only storyboards and simple sound.

Rough cut: A first version of a movie, made with the real soundtrack and basic animation.

Storyboard: A series of pictures that tell the story of a TV show or movie. Used as a rough plan.

MAKE YOUR OWN ANIMATION

You can create simple animation by drawing a stick figure in a different position on each page of a notebook or notepad. When you flip the pages quickly, the image seems to move. The thicker the paper stock, the easier it will be to flip the pages. You can do the same thing with a simple video-editing program on a computer. Draw a simple character in different positions, then put them in order on the software's timeline and press play.

CRAYONS

Living Color

Crayons are a popular drawing tool for today's young artists. The average North American kid uses 730 of them by age ten. In 1903, an American chemical company invented crayons as we know them now. It took the basic wax crayon it already made for marking crates and barrels, and created a nontoxic version in different colors.

Crayons today are made from a mix of waxes—mostly one called paraffin. It's perfect because it's inexpensive and easy to melt. It also has what's called a nice "rub-off," meaning it leaves plenty of wax on the paper.

They tint the wax, mixing yellow and red to make orange crayons. This factory can make 127 different colors. They add more wax and blend the mixture for 45 minutes. Then they pump the mixture into a device called a rotary machine. It injects the wax into crayon-shaped molds, then surrounds the molds with cool water, hardening the wax in about a minute.

Workers in the factory melt the wax, then adds a secret powder to strengthen the crayon and act as a filler, boosting the number of crayons the wax will make. They also add synthetic chemicals, including one to keep the wax from sticking to the molds, and a fatty acid called **stearic acid** made from natural oils to improve rub-off.

Next, a blade scrapes off excess wax to recycle it. Just one rotary machine molds more than 2,700 crayons at a time. With several machines working together, the factory makes 30,000 crayons every hour. That's a lot of pictures of rocket ships and flowers!

The rotary machine being filled with the many crayon molds.

The machine spits out the crayons, and a conveyor brings them to a labeling machine. They fall into the grooves of a revolving drum. The machine adds glue, sticks a label on each crayon, and uses a roller to press it into place. It labels 8,500 crayons every hour.

The crayons leave the labeling machine and land in a bulk box. Workers sort them by color into the hoppers of a packing machine. The machine bundles them in packs of sixteen or twenty-four. If a box comes up a crayon short, the machine automatically blows it from the conveyor belt with a strong blast of air. A worker adds the missing crayon and the box goes back onto the belt, ensuring a full complement of colors for every budding artist.

Hey, I know that smell

The smell of crayons is one of the most well-known scents in the United States. A Yale study discovered it was one of the top eighteen odors they tested. The smell comes from stearic acid.

WORDS TO KNOW

Stearic acid: A fatty acid made from beef fat or vegetable oil that forms a waxy solid. It's used to harden crayons, soap bars, and candles.

FISHING RUBBINGS

Still Life with Bluegill

People who go fishing like to exaggerate the size of their catches. (Not you. We mean everybody else.) In nineteenth-century Japan, they used fish rubbings to prove their stories were legit. Anglers spread ink on their fish and pressed them onto paper to transfer a lasting image. They called this process **gyotaku**.

Today, fish rubbing has evolved into an art form. Why paint a picture when you can print it? To start, an artist traces a fish outline on a foam block, and cuts out a fish-shaped bowl to hold the fish in place. He tucks paper in the fish's mouth to keep it open for a more interesting print, and puts more paper under the gill flaps to stop leaks.

This artist will use pins to prop up the fins. He leaves them to dry in place overnight so the fish will look like it's swimming in the print. Then he makes his own paint **applicators** by wrapping makeup sponges around wine corks and taping them in place. They'll let him add ink smoothly, with no brush strokes. He makes a different applicator for each color, and a couple extra for blending different colors.

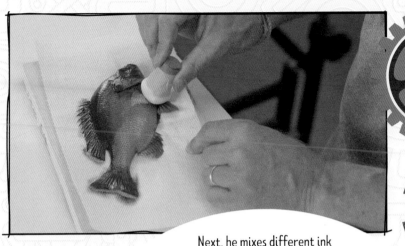

Next, he mixes different ink colors to get a shade that matches the fish's scales, blending in a little poppy seed oil to make it easier to brush. He puts a paper towel under the fish to protect the foam block from getting any paint on it. Then he pats greenish black paint on the gills and tail with a foam brush. He adds blue-green ink to the upper half, yellow to the belly, and red to the chest. He puts paper under a fin so he can coat it with green ink without getting any on the fish's yellow belly.

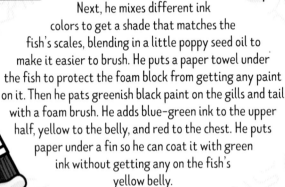

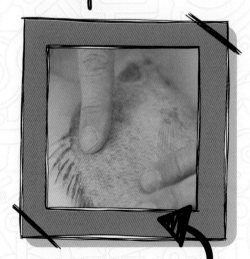

The artist rubbing the paper onto the painted fish.

He's now ready to make the print. He lightly sprays a sheet of rice paper with water to soften it. Then he gently presses every inch of the paper onto the fish with his fingertips to transfer the image. This takes skill and the right touch. Next he carefully peels off the paper. When the ink is dry, he lightly sprays it with more water, and then with water-based dye to add background color.

The paper is too flimsy for mounting, so the artist brushes wheat paste onto a second sheet. He wets the rubbing, and an assistant lowers it onto the paper. Meanwhile, the artist uses a soft brush to smooth out any wrinkles. Since the fish's eye didn't transfer, he paints one with black and yellow, adding a soulful expression. His work is now ready for mounting on more rigid paper. He trims the borders, tapes the rubbing to a mounting board, and signs it. It takes him weeks to make a fish rubbing like this, but this is one fish that will never get away.

WORDS TO KNOW

Applicator: A tool for applying something—often a liquid—to a surface.

Gyotaku: The Japanese art of creating paper rubbings from real fish.

MAKE YOUR OWN FISH RUBBING

You will need:
- Newspapers or old towels to protect the table
- A fish or a model of a fish
- Block printing inks
- Small plates to hold the ink
- A small hand-roller or handmade cork-and-sponge applicators
- Paper

1. Place the towels or newspaper on your work surface
2. Wash and dry the fish.
3. Pour some ink into the plates.
4. Roll the roller through the ink.
5. Roll an even coat of paint onto the fish.
6. Press the fish onto the paper, using even pressure.
7. Experiment with different color paints.

7

VEHICLES

Thousands of years ago, someone wondered, *How can I get from one place to another easier?* The answer came in two parts—the wheel and the pack animal. Since then, people keep asking how to travel farther, faster, cheaper, and more safely, all while carrying more things. Today, the airplane and tow truck are just a few of the ways we get from here to there. We've even got some just-for-fun ways, like mountain bikes and high-end motorcycles. Let's look at how innovators, designers, and workers make some of the many rolling, flying, skimming vehicles we use today.

ALUMINUM AIRCRAFT

Metal Fliers

Small airplanes need to be strong to stand up to the wear and tear of frequent flying, or landing on rugged grass airstrips instead of smooth, paved runways. Aluminum is sturdy and lightweight—that's why it's a favorite for building aircraft. The airplane you see here has a pressurized cabin, so it can fly at up to thirty thousand feet. It also has a deicing system for the wings, tail, and propeller, so it can fly safely in freezing weather.

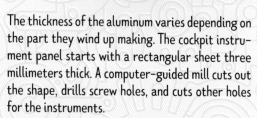

At the aircraft factory, workers unroll big aluminum sheets and feed them through a machine that flattens them with rollers. Then a cutting tool automatically slices them to specific lengths.

The thickness of the aluminum varies depending on the part they wind up making. The cockpit instrument panel starts with a rectangular sheet three millimeters thick. A computer-guided mill cuts out the shape, drills screw holes, and cuts other holes for the instruments.

The front edge of each wing, known as the leading edge, starts with a large rectangular sheet. Workers feed it between the rollers of a machine that bends it to a specific **radius**.

The leading edge is made of lots of metal parts. To stick them all together, the workers coat them with solvent, lay them on a sheet of **epoxy** glue, and cut the sheet with a utility knife. That gives the parts a sticky backing.

They use metal clamps to hold the parts together on a kind of rack called a bonding fixture. They build the leading edge part by part, then add a thin but strong and shiny metal skin. Next, they heat the whole thing in an oven so the glue sticks everything together.

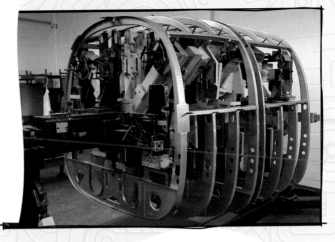

Clear runway five, because we're getting closer! Another team builds the frame for the main section of the plane—called the **fuselage**. They load the metal sheets onto another fixture and rivet them together, filling the gaps with sealant. They have to make the plane's skin airtight so passengers can breathe at thirty thousand feet. There's not much air up there! They add the aluminum skin, holding it with special fasteners called clecos while they rivet it in place.

The workers build the fuselage in six sections. They rivet the sections together, then add a big piece called a spar that holds the wings. They add retractable landing gear, the tail rudder and stabilizers, and moving panels called **flaps** and **ailerons** to let the pilot make the plane go left and right or up and down.

Now it's time to add the engine. Welders use steel tubes to build a sturdy engine mount. They prime and paint the finished mount, then bolt the five-hundred-horsepower turbine engine to it, and install it in the plane. Vroom!

Easy fixing

Because the aluminum skin of the airplane has lots of panels, it's easy to repair. Workers can just remove a damaged panel and replace it with a new one.

The plane needs miles of wiring to power and control its many systems. The workers put the wiring together like a big string puzzle before they add it to the plane. They tie the wire together on a big board, into a web of wiring called a **wiring harness.** They install one of these harnesses behind the plane's **instrument panel.** The panel has three display screens. With the push of a button, the pilot can choose what she sees on each one.

They add "steering wheels," called yokes. There are two because the copilot needs one too. The workers test everything, including the autopilot system that will let the plane fly by itself on long trips so the pilots can take a rest. They add windows and seats, and paint the plane, adding a registration number required by law. Ready for takeoff!

The finished aircraft in the skies!

How airplanes fly

An airplane wing is formed in a special shape called an airfoil. It's curved at the leading edge and pointed at the back. As the engine moves the plane forward, the airfoil forces air down, pushing the plane up.

Thin air

As planes fly higher, air gets thinner. That makes it easier to fly faster and farther, using less fuel. But that thin air makes it hard to breathe. To fix that, planes pump oxygen from metal tanks into a pressurized cabin. Snacks, anyone?

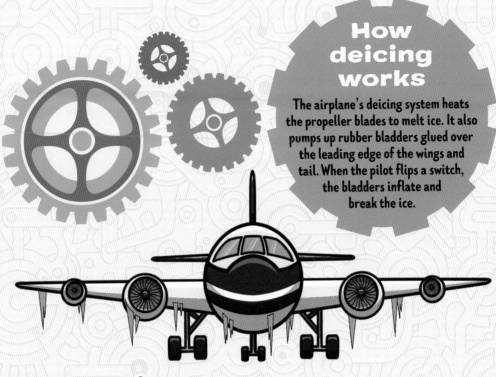

How deicing works

The airplane's deicing system heats the propeller blades to melt ice. It also pumps up rubber bladders glued over the leading edge of the wings and tail. When the pilot flips a switch, the bladders inflate and break the ice.

WORDS TO KNOW

Ailerons: Small hinged sections of a wing used to deflect air upward or downward. Controlled from the cockpit and usually motorized.

Epoxy: A sticky resin, often in two parts that are mixed or heat-treated to create a permanent bond.

Flaps: Hinged parts on a wing used to slow the aircraft during takeoff or landing.

Fuselage: The main body of an airplane, without the wings.

Instrument Panel: The dashboard in front of the pilot that contains the gauges, screens, and controls that let the pilot fly the plane.

Radius: The distance from the center of a curve to its edge.

Wiring harness: The web of electrical wiring in a motor vehicle like a car, motorcycle, or airplane that transmits power and electrical signals.

HELICOPTERS

Vertical Fliers

When it comes to flying, helicopters are the perfect go-anywhere machines. They can zip you around the sea cliffs of Hawaii or take you skiing in the Himalayas. Unlike airplanes, helicopters can move in almost any direction and they don't need runways. Now that we've got your attention, let's see what goes into building these amazing flying machines.

Plans for a helicopter are created on a computer, using 3-D design software. Then the workers shape the outer parts by layering carbon fiber—a **composite** fabric that's lighter and stronger than steel. They add a plastic coating to protect it, and cut it with a blade controlled by ultrasound. They build the rear fuselage with several carbon fiber layers, using a laser to position the parts. Then they add curved panels, molding them in place with a heat gun, and bake the whole assembly in a big, round, pressurized oven to harden it.

To make the door that covers the motor, they clamp more carbon fiber in a holder called a cutting jig. Then they shape it with hand tools.

This helicopter will have almost 1.5 miles of wires to control its many systems, but other helicopters can have 6 miles of wiring. Talk about a tangle! To keep things straight, they add the wires to a patterned wooden board one by one to make a complicated wiring harness.

Workers apply a sealant to the helicopter's outside parts to prevent corrosion, then put the fuselage together bit by bit, and rivet everything in place. It takes almost 10,000 rivets to build this helicopter. After this, they install a 260-pound motor and a circular plate that holds the helicopter's long, spinning blades. Then they bolt the blades in place, which are made of **composites** and aluminum.

They install the dashboard and control panel next, and hook up all the wiring. Last, they add seats, safety belts, inner walls called **bulkheads**, windows, doors, and all the trimmings. Then they paint the helicopter and test it to make sure it's ready to zip you up among the clouds.

The finished motor ready to be installed!

It takes 110 days to build an airship like this out of more than 3,000 parts. The factory makes 185 of them each year.

Fast bird

This helicopter can fly as high as 20,000 feet at speeds of up to 140 knots, or 160 mph. Knot is short for "nautical miles." One knot is about 1.15 mph.

WORDS TO KNOW

Bulkhead: A structural wall or partition in a vehicle, like a helicopter or ship.

Composites: Ultra-strong material made of fiber and resin.

MOUNTAIN BIKES

Rock Hoppers

Where did mountain bikes come from? In the late 1800s, the American military wanted bicycles that soldiers could ride on rough terrain. After that, smart people kept improving the designs, adding good ideas for decades. Today, these go-anywhere vehicles are real fan favorites. Their special suspension keeps the wheels in contact with the ground no matter how bumpy the trail. Deep-treaded tires add traction, and powerful **disc brakes** help you stop in a flash when a tree jumps out in front of you.

At each bike's core is a small, strong frame made from tubes of light, inexpensive aluminum alloy. Workers cut the tubes, put them in a rack called a jig, and **tack weld** them together. Then a welding machine completes the welds. To make the metal easier to work with, they treat each frame with intense heat, followed by a cool bath. The welding warps the metal a bit, so the workers tap it back in place with a rubber mallet. Then they heat it again to lock it into shape.

Once in a while, they use machines to test a finished frame, simulating ten years of *True Grit*-style slamming and vibration in three days. They want to make sure you won't break your bike when you huck it off a kicker.

The workers bore out the tubes, spray on auto-grade paint, and dry it in an oven. They use ink-transfer tape to add the logo, and spray on a clear coat of varnish.

An assembler adds an oil-filled rear shock absorber and the handlebars. He installs a rear brake **caliper** too. It works by squeezing brake fluid through a skinny tube, clamping the caliper against a disk attached to the wheel.

Next come the **crankset** and **derailleurs**. The crankset is the cog the pedals will attach to. Derailleurs push the chain from one sprocket to the next whenever you shift gears. The result? You won't slow down on tough trails where quick gear changes are needed. The technician adds a rear wheel with ten cogs and a disc brake, and screws in the front brake caliper.

It takes about an hour to fully build this mountain bike, but it'll last for years. Get ready for those berms and booters, rock jock.

Oil shocks

A mountain bike's shock absorbers are filled with oil to dampen impacts. This way the suspension doesn't bounce up and down and jar your teeth.

WORDS TO KNOW

Caliper: On a bicycle, the part of the brake that pinches the pad into the wheel rim or the disc.

Crankset: A set of one or more sprockets on a bike. The rider uses them to turn the wheels by pedaling the pedals.

Disc brakes: Brakes that work by pressing a pad against a disc on the wheel.

Derailleurs: The part of a bicycle that changes gears by switching the chain from one sprocket to the next.

Tack weld: A small, temporary bond that holds or "tacks" two pieces of metal together.

HIGH-END
MOTORCYCLES

Two-Wheeled Speed

During the Great Depression, motorcycles were a cheap way to get around. But these days, a motorcycle can be a high-performance work of art. The sleek, shiny motorcycle you see here was made from custom-designed parts for a high-paying customer.

Production starts with a design on a computer, when an artist draws the motorcycle on a digital pad to make a blueprint. The manufacturer uses computerized tools, following the blueprint like a recipe, carving most of the parts from blocks of aircraft-grade aluminum. One exception—they build the exhaust system from welded pipes of stainless steel.

Next comes an ignition coil mount—a part that holds the coil of copper wire that makes a spark inside the engine. A probe scans it to find the center, and a software-driven cutter etches artwork into the black aluminum.

A technician installs a hundred-horsepower, **fuel-injected** V-twin engine in the bike's steel frame. He then mounts a six-speed **transmission** system to the engine so the rider can shift gears when laying down a rubber road.

He slides a part called a steering stem into the frame and screws a bearing to the top to hold it in place. The steering stem will connect the motorcycle's front wheel to the handlebars. He screws a nut onto the bearing to hold everything in place. He adds parts called triple clamps to the top and bottom of the steering stem. These triple clamps will hold the bike's shocks in place, to provide a nice, smooth ride when going over bumps.

Next, the technician adds an axle and a carbon fiber front wheel, tightening it in place with shiny titanium nuts. Now we can go, but what about stopping? He connects a six-piston brake system to the suspension fork and tightens the bolts.

He attaches handlebars with gauges, controls, and side-view mirrors. He connects the electronics and adds a small, curved hood called a **cowling** in front of the handlebars. It pushes air away from the rider and the engine, to keep you from getting bugs squashed in your teeth.

The worker adds a gleaming, two-piece aluminum gas tank for extra capacity and frame strength. Each half is carved from a solid metal bar and takes more than sixty hours to create. He installs belt drive pulleys that will transfer power from the transmission to the back wheel. He adds the shiny belt-drive cover and foot pegs, and this stylish street machine is ready for the open road. It took two weeks to make and costs more than many cars, but it isn't for the budget crowd. Let's rev it up and roll out.

Record ride

The world record motorcycle ride was 2,023 miles in 24 hours, set by Matthew McKelvey in 2014. Bet his back was tired!

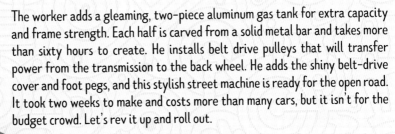

WORDS TO KNOW

Cowling: A removable cover on the front of a motorcycle or an airplane.

Fuel injection: A way to shoot a fine mist of fuel directly into an engine.

Transmission: A machine inside a vehicle that transmits power from the engine to the wheels or propeller.

TOW TRUCKS

Help on Wheels

When your car breaks down, you call a tow truck. But who do you call when a big truck breaks down? Answer: a *bigger* tow truck! The one you see here can haul a tractor-trailer out of a ditch. It has four strong legs it can extend to keep from falling over, and a thick pole called a recovery boom to give it a long reach. It's made of 2,500 parts cut from steel sheets by two computer-guided machines: a high-pressure water-jet cutter and a laser cutter.

Workers put the many metal parts of the tow truck's back—called the tow body—on an assembly **fixture**, then temporarily tack weld them together. A welding robot finishes the job, making a more permanent connection. They sandblast the parts to clean them, then paint them with protective primer.

A computer-guided high-pressure water jet cutter cutting a steel sheet!

Next, they connect powerful hydraulics and assemble the recovery boom. They install hydraulic cylinders to move the boom up and down, a winch that holds thick tow cables, and a giant ring gear that will rotate the boom in all directions. Then they connect the finished boom to the deck with massive steel pins. They attach the **underlift** at the back to let the truck hook onto the front wheels of other trucks, and four strong outriggers to keep the truck from falling over during rescue mode.

Now the towing deck is ready, but the workers have to connect it to the truck body. They weld big steel mounting plates to a prebuilt truck, then bolt the towing deck to the plates. They also add aluminum tool cabinets. In the rearmost cabinet, they add wiring for emergency lights and other gear.

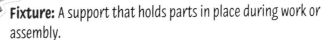

They install the driver's control panel and control handles last. After a full round of tests, this baby is ready for the road.

WORDS TO KNOW

Fixture: A support that holds parts in place during work or assembly.

Underlift: A lift that extends from the bottom of a tow truck, usually fitting under the front or back wheels of the towed vehicle.

FLYING WATER BIKES

Lake to the Skies

Looking to boost your game on the water? You literally can with a flying water bike. A fire hose attaches this streamlined flying bike to the back of a Jet Ski. Water shoots from the Jet Ski's water jet through the hose and out through the bike's jet nozzles. The powerful jet can thrust you up almost forty feet above the water, where you can flip and spin and dive.

The bike's frame is made from lightweight, rust-resistant aluminum. The bike also has three jet nozzles. One nozzle pushes the bike up. The other two turn it left or right.

To build the lifting-jet nozzle, a worker puts a metal tube around a post called an alignment fixture, then hammers an end cap on, welding it in place. He welds on a curved tube, a jet nozzle cone, and a handlebar too. He paints the new assembly to protect it, roughing it up first to help the paint stick by tumbling it with scratchy synthetic stones.

A pipe shaped like a T will send the jet of water to the control nozzles. A worker welds the T-part to the lifting jet and adds more metal parts for extra strength. He welds on a seat support, and sprays all the parts with thick, black powder paint. Then it's into an oven to bake the powder to a shiny finish.

144

A worker adds a locking part called a cam that will hold the fire hose in place. Another worker screws on foot plates to give you a place to put your feet when you take off. He bolts on parallel support bars and adds a comfy, padded knee rest.

He connects the jet control nozzle to the frame with screws and with three rings made of plastic and metal. Now it's time to put the bike's body together. It's made of molded plastic with waterproof cushions. The seat is completely watertight so it will keep the bike afloat. The last step is to bolt the body to the frame.

The completed water bike weighs just thirty pounds once it's connected to a fire hose, and it can fly at up to twenty miles per hour. By aiming the nozzles, you can do backflips, spins, and even dive twenty feet beneath the waves.

How to fly a bike

To make the bike go up, you pull back slowly on the handlebars. To go down, you push forward. To spin, you move one forward and one back. To do a backflip, you yank them both all the way back, hard. Hold on tight!

145

PONTOON BOATS

Shindig Ships

A pontoon boat is a fun way to get out on a lake, river, or bay. They make great platforms for water-skiing, wakeboarding, swimming, diving, exploring, or just grilling a few burgers and playing fetch with your pooch.

The air-filled chambers that make them float start as aluminum sheets. A rolling machine forms them into tubes, pressing with the weight of twenty-six elephants. A worker slides each one on a track so a welding machine can make a water-tight seal.

Another rolling machine shapes the nose cones. They're made of a special aluminum alloy that makes them shockproof, for when you want to bump them up on shore for a quick picnic. The cone parts are welded by hand in a process called **TIG welding** that can reach 9,000°F. Yikes!

The pontoons themselves are made of several round aluminum chambers. Each chamber has a wall on the end called a **baffle** that keeps leaks from filling the entire pontoon. A hydraulic press squeezes these chambers together for an extra-snug fit. Then a welder connects them and adds metal supports to hold up the boat's floor.

Pontoon boats were invented by a farmer in Minnesota named Ambrose Weeres. He made the first one by building a wooden deck on two rows of steel barrels. He turned his idea into a business that sold forty of his boats the next year.

Assemblers bolt crossbars to the supports with an air-powered wrench. They build the floor from sheets of pressure-treated plywood that won't rot when it gets wet. Pop rivets fasten the floor to the crossbars. Assemblers then cut and glue on a special rot-resistant marine carpet to keep you comfy when you're soaking up the rays.

The workers add fade-resistant decals to the aluminum side walls, and crimp them with rollers to make them stronger. They rivet them to the railings, then use a shaping machine to curve the railings for the corners. They screw and bolt the railings and furniture to the floor, adding a control console with buttons for the horn, lights, and music. And of course they add a throttle and a steering wheel.

Wires and control cables connect the captain's console to a fifty-horsepower motor. It won't win the Indy 500, but it gives a pontoon boat all the power it needs for a leisurely spin on the lake. Who packed the sandwiches?

WORDS TO KNOW

Baffle: A wall between two sections of a pontoon that seals the section. It stops a leak in one section from filling the entire pontoon.

TIG welding: An electrical arc-welding method using tungsten inert gas to join pieces of metal.

8

JUST FOR FUN

Now you've had a glimpse behind the scenes in factories that make electronics, musical instruments, sports gear, vehicles, and food. You've even seen how artists make their art. Now let's look at some purely fun products that make our world a better place. It's time to turn the page to learn how they make exciting things like gemstones, sparklers, swords, binoculars, and wooden matches. Here we go!

SPARKLERS

Handheld Fireworks

Sparklers have sizzled on the party scene for decades, adding pyrotechnic glitter to millions of backyard barbecues and festivals. They evolved from more traditional fireworks and are the only kind you can hold in your hand while they burn. This splash of flash can last a minute or more depending on the length of the metal wire inside.

Sparklers start with steel wires that get bundled and loaded into slots in a sorting machine. The machine vibrates and the wires fall into smaller openings. An operator moves a spring-loaded wooden rack that opens like an accordion. He rocks the machine, making the wires drop into little holes. After three hundred wires fall into place, he pulls a handle to close the rack.

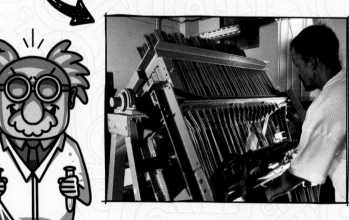

At the next station, a worker mixes chemicals called **boric acid** and **barium nitrate** in a big tank. He adds water and cornstarch, and fine iron filings to give the sparklers their golden sparks. Then he suits up in protective gear and shuts the door. He's the only one allowed to load the most volatile ingredient— aluminum powder.

Chain conveyors move the rack of sparkler wires into place. An elevator lifts the tank with the finished mixture up to dip and coat them. Almost 150 racks of wires get dipped each hour. They dry off in an oven, then get dipped again to make them thicker. After another baking and a quick inspection, they sit for a week to cure. Now they're ready to be packaged for your birthday party. It's time to ooh and ahh.

Freshly dipped wires drying.

Glowing tradition

The first fireworks were invented in the Song dynasty in China around the year 1000.

Big show

Wires for parade sparklers are a long thirty-six inches. They're heavier than ordinary sparklers, but they're worth it for their four-minute burn time.

WORDS TO KNOW

Barium nitrate: An inorganic compound that burns with a green flame. Commonly used in fireworks production.

Boric acid: A widely used chemical used to make textile fiberglass for computer circuit boards and boats, and for making fireworks.

WOODEN MATCHES

Fire on a Stick

People have been using fire for several hundred thousand years, but the invention of matches is fairly recent. The first matches were made in the fifth century in northern China. But commercial safety matches came on the scene only about one hundred years ago.

Before we can make the matches, we'll need a box to put them in. A roll feeds paper into a machine, and a hot iron dries out the paper. The machines in this factory can make one thousand boxes every minute! They cut, fold, glue, and shoot out a little rainbow arc of inner boxes onto a conveyor belt.

The conveyor drops the boxes into storage bins. Then another machine sorts them into single rows and stands them upright for a filling machine.

Now we need the matches. A worker pours **gelatin** capsules over a chemical called **potassium chlorate** in a mixer. The gelatin will stick the flammable chemicals to the match heads. He adds hot water to dissolve the capsules, then silica granules—like sand—to keep the matches from burning up too quickly. He rinses the mixer with water while it mixes. After forty minutes, he adds red coloring and other chemicals to help the match heads burn.

Now we need the matchsticks. The factory splinters wood from aspen trees into a matchstick shape. They soak the sticks with **ammonium phosphate** so they won't relight like trick birthday candles after you blow them out. A machine shakes off excess wood, and feeds over two million of these splints per hour into little holes in a special dipping sheet. The splints get dipped in **paraffin**, then into the match-head liquid.

Match heads freshly dipped in the paraffin.

It takes about an hour to dry the matches. Then a filling machine dumps two hundred of them every second into liner boxes. Next come outer boxes—called the skillets. Those are made the same way as the liners, but with printed writing and abrasive striking strips. A machine pushes the match-filled insert boxes inside the skillets, and the matches are ready to light your fire.

WORDS TO KNOW

Ammonium phosphate: A highly unstable compound with the chemical formula $(NH_4)_3PO_4$. More-stable forms are widely used in soldering flux and fertilizers.

Gelatin: A mix of proteins and other compounds taken from the bones, skin, and other tissues of industrially farmed animals like chickens, fish, and cows.

Paraffin: A waxy mix of hydrocarbons used in making candles and other products.

Potassium chlorate: A highly flammable chemical compound made of potassium, chlorine, and oxygen in the chemical formula $KClO_3$.

153

SWORDS

En Garde!

How would you like to swing a sword during a big battle in a castle, fighting enemies in clanking armor? Swords have been around for more than five thousand years, but making them is not a lost art. Modern artists still go to the hilt to make these sharp, intimidating weapons today.

The first step? An artisan lays a piece of high-carbon steel in a fixture. Then computer-guided blades carve out the shape of the sword. Centuries ago, a blacksmith would have done this tricky job by hand, but this machine is much faster and creates a more consistent cut. After about an hour, a nicely tapered sword blank emerges.

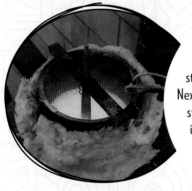

The blank is submerged in hot liquid salt—a critical step that softens the steel, removing stresses that were added during carving. Next, it's plunged into cool liquid in a sizzling step called **quenching**. The edge hardens immediately, but the center cools more slowly. This makes the sword more flexible, so it doesn't snap the next time you fight a dragon.

Sword makers use belt sanders to fine-tune the blade's shape in a shower of sparks. The blade is now sharp enough to cut paper, but strong enough to chop deep into a metal barrel without chipping.

154

Next, they pump wax into molds to make historically accurate copies of the hilt parts, called the guard and the **pommel**. The guard protects your hands, and the pommel is the bottom-weight that balances the sword. The workers use the wax copies to cast the parts in metal. Then they smooth and polish them.

They add a handle guard to the sword, cushioning it with plastic. A worker pounds it with a sledgehammer to whack it into place. He adds the pommel and a small, locking piece of steel called a peen block. Heating the peen block with a welding torch, he hammers it to flatten it. This locks the pommel, handle, and guard together as a single piece.

Ancient weapon

The oldest sword on record was made 5,300 years ago. The invention of the sword allowed countries to defend themselves against invaders. That gave them time to develop other technologies around food, communication, and transportation.

He glues two wooden grips to the handle with epoxy, clamping them. When the glue is dry, he glues black-dyed leather to the grips. He binds it with cord to squeeze it while it dries.

A sword maker uses chemicals to etch the maker's mark on the blade. Now you have a replica that's true to the medieval original. Clang! You're ready to fight off a whole crowd of trolls and ogres.

WORDS TO KNOW

Pommel: A counterweight at the base of a sword handle that makes it easier to manage.

Quench: To dip hot metal into cool water to harden it. The metal is often heated again, then allowed to air-cool slowly to add flexibility.

BINOCULARS

Close Vision

Binoculars are basically two little telescopes stuck together. They're also a great way to see lions and tigers on your next safari without getting close enough to wind up as a snack.

Each pair of binoculars starts with light-bending chunks of specially cut glass called **prisms**. Workers glue the prisms to steel plates using UV-light-activated glue, so a machine can grind and polish them with diamond dust. This fine polishing will reduce reflection—critical for making the glass see-through.

Next, the workers join two pieces of the glass using more UV glue. A special metal holding fixture ensures the angle is just right.

UV glue

Most of the glue in this factory is activated by an ultraviolet light. The light dries the glue instantly before the workers move on to the next step.

Now for the **objectives**. Those are the big, curved lenses at the front of the binoculars. They get ground and polished just like the prisms, then go through a nine-stage computer-guided cleaning process. After inspecting the lenses, a technician glues two of them together. This step stops fringes of color from popping up around the image when you zoom in on a kangaroo or Sherman tank.

A machine projects a dot of light on each lens, and a technician matches up the dots to line up the lenses perfectly. Another technician loads mineral pellets in a vacuum chamber. The pellets will give the glass an antireflection coating to let more light through. In a vacuum chamber, a beam of electrons evaporates the little pellets into tiny particles that coat the lenses.

It's time to put these peepers together. First, workers clean the lenses with compressed gas. They screw and glue them to the housing, which is made of plastic, aluminum, or carbon. They attach the smaller eyepiece lenses the same way.

The workers seal the housing with airtight silicon, then a machine sucks the air out and replaces it with **nitrogen** gas. Nitrogen keeps the lenses from fogging up while you're looking at the stars and planets on a chilly night. After being tested for vibration, water pressure, extreme heat, and freezing, these far-seeing eyes are ready for your next adventure.

How do binoculars work?

Light rays from an object enter the far end of the binoculars, where big lenses called objectives magnify the image and flip it upside-down. Prisms flip it right side up again, and smaller eyepiece lenses magnify it further. The first part of the prism rotates the image ninety degrees. The second turns it again, completing the flip.

WORDS TO KNOW

Nitrogen: An inert gas that makes up 78 percent of Earth's atmosphere. Ideal for use in sealed chambers like the inside of binoculars, because of its rust-inhibiting properties.

Objective lenses: The lenses at the front end of a pair of binoculars, through which the images enter.

Prism: A clear, solid shape that bends light. Some prisms are made specially to flip an image. Others split white light into all the colors of the spectrum.

FLEECE

Toasty Plastic

The fleece inside the jacket that keeps you warm on a cold day is made from used plastic bottles.

In the factory, a machine shreds the bottles into plastic chips. Pulses of hot air toss them, giving them hard shells that keep them from clumping together. A dryer blows out moisture that would weaken the final product. Then a worm screw moves the chips through heated pipes, melting them into a thick liquid. This molten recycled polyester is now ready to be turned into yarn.

A machine presses the plastic through a part called a die plate that has holes in it like a showerhead. It's part of a device called a spin pack, made of a mesh filter, a metal distribution plate, and bits of shattered metal to screen out impurities.

Workers heat the pack to keep the plastic soft. Then the plastic flows out through the holes in the die plate, cooling into strands five times thinner than a human hair. These funnel into a guide that bundles them, creating yarn. The yarn travels around rollers into a compartment where air buffets it to tangle up the strands. A spool winds up the yarn at a speed of 125 miles per hour.

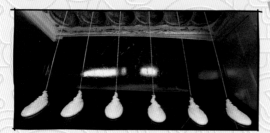

How fleece keeps you warm

Tiny fleece fibers trap air between them, just like the natural fibers of wool or cotton. That trapped air creates an insulating layer around your body. Unlike cotton, the fibers in fleece and wool don't flatten when you get them wet. That means they'll keep you toasty even when you're drenched.

The liquid polyester being filtered and shaped as filaments, hardening as they cool.

Recycled warmth

The polyester in plastic bottles comes from petroleum, so recycling means we can use a little more of this resource for other means.

Now a robot forklift picks up the spools for inspection. Other machines pull the new yarn over heated rubber rollers, stretching it. More equipment twists it and gathers it on spools again. It's woven together with wool yarn from sheep by high-speed knitting machines. Then it's dyed to different colors, and brushed by wire brushes to fluff it up. The process takes a couple weeks, but now the fleece is ready to be sewn into your next warm coat, to keep you toasty on the snow-swept slopes of Mount Yerupaja, or just your own backyard.

Polyester: A plastic made of petroleum-derived hydrocarbons, used to make clothing, bottles, conveyor belts, and thousands of other items.

SCREWDRIVERS

Turning Point

If you've ever built something out of wood, you've probably used a screwdriver. But have you ever wondered how they're made?

Making a screwdriver starts with coils of specially formulated steel. Wheels straighten it, and a machine cuts it and forces it through tools called dies.

The first die narrows the steel rod, and three more add a six-sided shape called a **bolster**. That shape will let you grip the screwdriver with a wrench to boost its turning power. A quick shower washes it, and workers check for defects. Next, the shafts head into a machine that flattens the tips, trims them, and stamps on a part number.

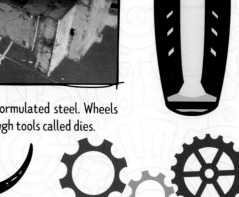

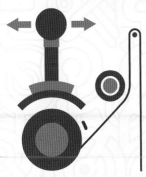

After the shafts are heat-treated to increase their hardness, the tips are sanded and shuttled over to a grinding wheel for subtle trimming. Then they twirl in a machine that blasts the tips with a mild **abrasive**. This adds texture to help them grip a screw head.

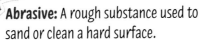

A press
slams into the far end
to make some grippy grooves.
Then an assembler adds a plastic handle,
and a machine pushes it onto the grooves.
Another machine adds plastic wrap and
shrinks it tight inside a furnace. Now
these screwdrivers are ready for all
kinds of twists and turns.

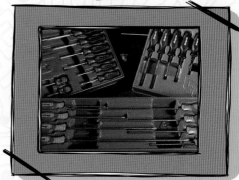

WORDS TO KNOW

Abrasive: A rough substance used to sand or clean a hard surface.

Bolster: A part that props up another part or holds it in place.

Lag time

Screwdrivers were invented in the Middle Ages, but didn't become popular until hundreds of years later.

161

SPECIAL EFFECTS SNOW

Movie Magic

Mother nature doesn't follow orders, so when a film or TV script needs a frosty blizzard or a gentle snowfall, moviemakers use a snow machine to make it. The flakes are actually tiny soap bubbles that only look like snow on camera. It might be blazing hot outside, but on the set, it's winter.

To make the flakes, workers mix sudsy chemicals like the ones in your shampoo. They add water, and then a machine pumps the mixture into jugs. Each one contains enough snow **concentrate** to make it snow for sixteen hours.

To build the snowmaking machine, a worker drills air holes in something called a snowhead. It's the part that spits out the fake flakes. He feeds wires through the snowhead for a blower fan, and tubes for the snow concentrate.

162

He bolts the snowhead to a blower and heat-shrinks the wires and tubes in plastic wrap. Another worker carves a hole in the blower's cover. He puts the snowhead in the hole, and ties the wires and tubes to the guard. Then he adds more brackets to help hang the machine high above a movie set. Snowdrifts, here we come!

He connects the fan, wires, and tubes, and fits a special sock over the snow-head. A pump will push the snowmaking liquid through the sock, straining it into a froth. The fan will blow the froth to make the snowflakes fly around. He adds the pump and a metal controller box, and weights the tube's free end to keep it in the snow solution. Now the fun part. A technician tests everything by making it snow for hours. We're now ready to whip up an instant blizzard. "Action!"

Whoops!

The makers of the movie *The Holiday* rented a snowmaking machine. They didn't know it would snow three times during their week of filming.

WORDS TO KNOW

Concentrate: A thick liquid mixed with a thinner liquid like water to create a final product.

163

GEMSTONES

Sparkling Stones

Genuine gemstones come from minerals, rocks, or even organic materials shaped and polished. The rarest ones are classified as precious gems. Others are called semiprecious. The semiprecious stone you see here—called Blue John—is a type of fluoride, like the fluoride in your toothpaste. It has bands of purple, blue, and yellow. It's found in only one place in the world: the village of Castleton, Derbyshire, in central England.

The stone comes from a cavern 165 feet beneath a hillside. The miners don't use explosives because the stone is soft and brittle, and would shatter. They use drills instead to carefully dislodge it.

They carry the Blue John to a surface workshop where more workers wash off clay and dirt. It's been under wet ground for 240 million years, so they dry it in an oven at low heat for a couple weeks. The stone is still brittle, so they dunk it in a bowl of liquid resin. The resin will soak into all the pores and harden it. When they're done, they dry it in another oven.

Artisans turn the stone on a lathe, working it slowly with diamond-tipped tools. Diamond is harder than all other rocks, so it cuts cleanly and easily. Workers saw the stone into slices with a diamond-edged saw, and send the slices to a jewelry shop.

Now a **silversmith** creates a piece of jewelry—in this case a sterling silver ring. She bends and solders the ring's ends together. She grinds the solder flat and fuses on a **setting** to hold the jewel. She gives it a good polishing to make it shine.

A **gemologist** examines slices of Blue John in a light box that shows up any flaws. She cuts out a gemstone shape, and glues on a backing cut from a shiny substance called mother-of-pearl. It's taken from the shells of oysters and other **mollusks**, and it brings out the colors in the gemstone.

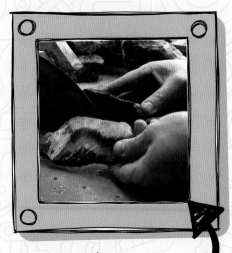

Gemstone being sliced with a diamond-edged saw.

165

The gemologist shapes the gemstone with a diamond-grit grinding wheel to make a perfect fit. Then she glues it firmly into the ring's setting. She sands the edges into a sleek dome called a "cabochon." Then she polishes the ring surface until the silver and Blue John glisten and sparkle. Now this piece of gorgeous jewelry is ready to make you shine.

Versatile gemstone

Blue John is also used to make large items like goblets and bowls.

Rarer than diamonds

One of the rarest gemstones on Earth is ammolite—found in the Rocky Mountains. It's made from shells of ancient mollusk fossils more than sixty-five million years old. The gem shimmers with many of the colors of the rainbow.

WORDS TO KNOW

Fluoride: A type of mineral used in toothpaste, manufacturing, and jewelry production.

Gemologist: A specialist who works with and judges the value of gems.

Mollusk: A creature with no bones that often has a shell. Examples are oysters, snails, mussels, and octopuses.

Setting: A metal holder for a gemstone in a piece of jewelry.

Silversmith: A metal worker who crafts items from silver, such as rings, necklaces, and flatware.

CONCLUSION

Now that you know *how it's made*, what ideas do *you* have? What questions do you have that you think you can answer with new ideas? What problems do you see that you think you could solve? Could you build a better mousetrap, gummy vitamin, or telescope? Or do you have an idea for a product that we haven't covered yet in the book or on the show? To learn more about how everyday items are made, head over to www.sciencechannel.com/show/how-its-made-science to watch more episodes!